MW01026808

PRAISE FOR
The Art of Alignment

"The key to great interviewing is listening—concentrating solely on the answer to be sure you're aligned with your guest. The same is true for great business leaders. Art's guide for gaining greater alignment can help any team or organization achieve top performance."

—Larry King,
The world's most recognized interviewer

"This book is about helping you develop the strategic leadership skills necessary to achieve higher performance through the individuals who make up your organization. Reading it is like taking an MBA course in workplace performance. Implementing the strategies within these pages is bound to enhance your career as a leader and generate incredible results for your organization."

—Harvey Mackay,
Author of *Pushing the Envelope All the Way to the Top*

"Today's best organizations need alignment, not just engagement, to drive their success. *The Art of Alignment* shows leaders how to identify, achieve and sustain organizational alignment to fulfill their mission and goals."

—Ken Blanchard,
Co-Author of *The New One-Minute Manager*
and *Servant Leadership in Action*

"As a fraternity of excellence, it is paramount for Alphas to be aligned with our mission of leadership, brotherhood, academic achievement, and community advocacy. Following *The Art of Alignment* will help us achieve our strategic goals and increase our community impact."

—Dr. Willis Lonzer III,
General President, Alpha Phi Alpha Fraternity, Inc.*

*Established in 1906, Alpha Phi Alpha is the nation's first intercollegiate historically African-American fraternity. Open to men of all races since 1945, Alpha Phi Alpha today has more than 800 chapters globally and nearly 300,000 members.

"The creativity and individual initiative of our employees is a foundation of our innovation model. *The Art of Alignment* outlines and drives home the importance of creativity and empowerment within an aligned organization to match performance with purpose."

—John Banovetz, CTO, 3M

"This is an exceptional book for anyone aspiring to be a CEO. The art of management has evolved over time in many ways. Leadership has become more complex recently with the issues of diversity, inclusion, globalization, and ESG. This book provides a roadmap with various details, ideas, and references on how to lead successful, effective organizations."

—Rear Admiral James B. Whittaker,
U.S. Navy (retired) and Author of
Strategic Planning in a Rapidly Changing Environment

"When leading sales-driven organizations, getting teams to align with a company's mission and vision is a game-changer. If you're seeking answers for creating a high-performance team, look no further. Use the strategies in this book as your guide."

—Tom Hopkins,
Best-selling Author of *How to Master the Art of Selling*

"Law enforcement officers who fully embrace the mission and vision of their office will work diligently to enhance public trust. *The Art of Alignment* brings forth the key concepts and practices that we have used to align our office and pursue better business practices."

—Sheriff James Stuart,
Anoka County, MN and Secretary of
the National Sheriffs' Association

"When Art and I worked together at USWest, I saw how his grasp of alignment to mission and vision had the power to create something great. *The Art of Alignment* is the culmination of the learnings and practice he developed and grew over time."

—John Kelley,
Chairman & CEO, CereHealth Corp.

"As Chief Legal Officer for a major insurance company, maintaining alignment to our mission and purpose was critical to achieving success in the face of exacting regulatory requirements. Art's book does a great job of helping leaders understand how they can better lead and align their organizations."

—Wayne Robinson,
Former Chief Legal Officer (retired),
Allianz Life Insurance Company of North America

"When I was CEO of Watson Wyatt Worldwide, I pushed hard with SHRM to include alignment issues as part of their certification process. *The Art of Alignment* does a great job of not only outlining the core pillars of alignment but showing how to practice the techniques and measure the impact."

—Pete Smith,
CEO, Watson Wyatt Worldwide (retired)

"I depend on aligned employees to keep us innovative and ensure our customer's best experience. *The Art of Alignment* does a great job outlining ways to keep that innovation and creativity at the core of aligning a company's mission and vision. Highly recommended."

—Jennifer Smith,
President & CEO, Innovative Office Solutions

"As I was watching my father, Herb Brooks, lead the 1980 US Olympic Hockey team to Gold, I saw firsthand how alignment to mission and vision conquered the toughest foes. *The Art of Alignment* shows how you can align your organization in ways to drive success. "

—Dan Brooks,
Managing Director of RBC Wealth Management and son of legendary Olympic Hockey Coach, Herb Brooks

The Art
of
Alignment

A DATA-DRIVEN APPROACH
TO LEAD ALIGNED ORGANIZATIONS

ART JOHNSON

Made for Success
PUBLISHING

Made for Success Publishing
P.O. Box 1775 Issaquah, WA 98027
www.MadeForSuccessPublishing.com

Distributed by Made for Success Publishing

First Printing

Library of Congress Cataloging-in-Publication data
Johnson, Art
      The Art of Alignment: A Data-Driven Approach to Lead Aligned
        Organizations
      p. cm.
      LCCN: 2020949766
      ISBN: 978-1-64146-492-5 *(hardback)*
      ISBN: 978-1-64146-538-0 *(ebook)*
      ISBN: 978-1-64146-539-7 *(audiobook)*

Printed in the United States of America

For further information contact Made for Success Publishing
+14255266480 or email service@madeforsuccess.net

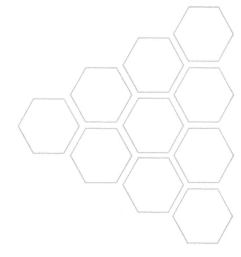

TABLE OF CONTENTS

"Leaders with influence:
Give more, take less
Care for others
Grow continuously
Live authentically
Empower others
Manage hardship
Serve with humility."

Napoleon Hill

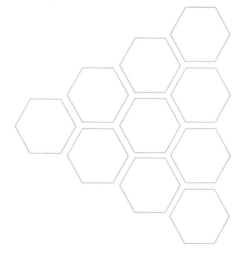

ACKNOWLEDGMENTS

I would like to acknowledge (more like exalt) my father for expanding my thinking by asking thought-provoking questions in response to my haphazard inquiry, rather than supplying a solitary perspective. His unique way of transferring knowledge and wisdom is indelibly etched in my brain, forever enhancing my creativity and quest for clarity.

A special thanks to Joe Byrd and Del Johnson, my brothers whom I lean on in troubled times, share my deepest thoughts with and count on for keeping me grounded.

John Kelley was a boss, mentor, and friend that took a chance on an up-and-coming executive with some decent instincts but rough around the edges. Rather than attempting to harness my enthusiasm, John encouraged risk-taking, which brilliantly complemented my "trial and error" approach to life. My confidence flourished.

Harvey Mackay's reputation and accomplishments extend beyond his literary work. His wisdom and generosity are only eclipsed by his pursuit of excellence in everything he does. This book's foreword is a small example of Harvey's reach.

Dr. Ken Bartlett was the first person to suggest that I write this book. His confidence in me and inspirational nudging was the tipping point in getting started.

Sean McDonnell's value to my team and this book can be summed up in one word: vital. Sean's keen eye for detail and his ability to capture sentiment and nuance with the right word in the right place is incomparable.

A special thanks to Erik Beckler, whom I count on for telling me the truth and picking up the ball when I toss it to him (or merely drop it). His contribution to this book is significant, and I appreciate his willingness to help where necessary and foster momentum.

Lastly, my advisory board has been inspirational when I was not at my best and constructively critical when my "creativity" ran askew. I truly trust and respect my advisors because, without their guidance and support, none of this would be possible.

To my readers, I hope this book provides a framework for measuring progress in an area we oft think about but seldom monitor. *The Art of Alignment* was not written to provide guardrails for leaders; instead, it should be considered an imperfect case study that continues to evolve with more data and analytical rigor. The stories should illuminate the pillars in a manner that expands leadership thinking and promotes constructive discourse. These pillars have worked for many leaders and can now help *you* achieve organizational alignment.

Good luck and Godspeed!

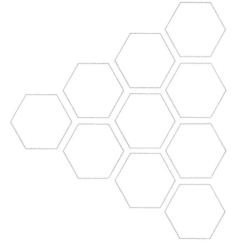

FOREWORD

Early in my career, I figured out that success in business is all about relationships. In fact, my Golden Rule of Selling is this: *Know Your Customer*. When it comes to being an effective leader, that saying translates to Know Your *People*. As a leader, this group includes your peers—the other leaders within the organization. Of course, your people are also those who report to you and, in most cases, team members who are several layers down the organizational chart. The more you know about the people in your organization, the better prepared you will be to place them well and encourage their performance.

I've had the privilege to see Art Johnson on the firing line one-on-one with a potential customer on several occasions. All I can say is I was glad Art was not working for my competition in the business of selling envelopes! His preparation, knowledge, street smarts, presentation skills, and uncommon wisdom were unparalleled. Oh yes, incidentally, he got the order!

Now, his attention is devoted to the skills leaders need to develop in order to drive alignment within their organizations. I am excited about this because every person I know who has interfaced with Art does not just *like* him … they *love* him. If his company were publicly owned, I'd call my broker and get my hands on all the stock I could buy at the market price.

As the world of business evolves, it is extraordinarily important for leaders to acknowledge that there is—and always will be—more to learn. The biggest room in the world is the room for improvement. When your leadership skills improve, it only makes sense that those you lead will respond better.

Leadership in itself is a broad category. It requires strategic thinking, creativity, excellent communication skills, consistency, and humility. Wise leaders hire and inspire brilliant people to get the job done, then basically get out of their way—providing strategic plans and guidance to keep the organizational "ship" on course.

With the ability of today's businesses to readily capture and analyze all sorts of data, tools have been developed to spot the challenges organizations face. Data tells us what's going on, then it's up to us, as leaders, to figure out why and make course adjustments, as necessary.

As with any type of challenge, the first step to overcoming it is to admit you have a problem. The key to success in organizations then becomes one of transparency and trust. Being open about challenges and encouraging everyone involved to contribute to solutions is the way to go. It leads to having an organization of individuals who are aligned around a common cause and wanting to perform at their highest levels.

That's what this book is all about—helping you develop the strategic leadership skills necessary to achieve higher performance through the individuals who make up your organization. Reading it is like taking an MBA course in workplace performance. Implementing the strategies within these pages is bound to enhance your career as a leader and generate incredible results for your organization.

Harvey Mackay
Author of *Pushing the Envelope All the Way to the Top* and *You Haven't Hit Your Peak Yet!*

7

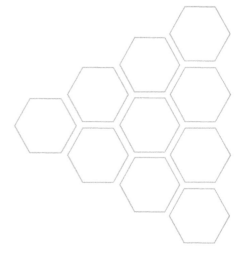

INTRODUCTION

There's a certain thrill in taking on new leadership challenges. Challenges make you stretch and grow not only as a person but in your leadership skills as well. Being an effective leader, not only today but into the future, requires a commitment to continued growth. The challenges are never going to be the same. You must commit to doing your best and using the tools at your disposal at every given moment.

That was a lesson I learned early in life from my father. Whether it was when considering my report card or my performance as an athlete, his question was always the same, "Was that the best you could do?" Knowing I would be asked that question motivated me always to do my best—to give my all to whatever I was involved in. I didn't want to disappoint my father. But, more importantly, I didn't want to disappoint *myself*.

A few generations back, my ancestors were slaves, listed as "property" on the inventory of a plantation along with livestock, barns, and equipment. There was never a sense of entitlement in my family history. In the stories passed down through the generations, my people always worked hard. I was never afraid to do so, either.

After graduating from college, I was a marketing representative with IBM. I moved up the ranks quickly, always eager to take on more responsibilities. At one point, I became the manager in the North Central District/Midwest Trading Area for what was then known as the PC Company. The market for PCs was becoming quite competitive. Innovation was the name of the game, not only to gain market share but to consider the future of where it was going. It was determined that the best move was to spin off the manufacturing of printers and inks to meet market demands. That spin-off turned into Lexmark—manufacturer of printers and inks that became somewhat of a household name. I wasn't involved in that decision, but I learned a great deal from it. I learned that it was important to look at how an organization can continuously improve itself and expand how it meets its mission. There always needs to be an eye on the future.

Understanding the value of continued personal growth as a leader, I earned my master's degree in business administration. Upon earning that degree, I was recruited to work with US West Communications as the vice president of internet sales. My responsibilities included leading more than 2,000 employees with a billion dollars' worth of revenue responsibility. Talk about growing within a position! Having that many people look to you for leadership really causes you to step up your game.

Even when you do your best as a leader, there may be times when your only moves within an organization will be lateral. That happened to me. The challenges at US West became less dramatic, the opportunities for growth were limited, and others were promoted instead of me. So, I sought out new challenges elsewhere and took a position with Medtronic.

At the time, Medtronic, the world's largest medical device company, had to meet a goal of placing a diversity hire at the vice-presidential level. I was offered the challenge of improving sales in their Mountain Region. To say there were multiple challenges to address in taking on this position would be an understatement.

For starters:

1. No one had ever been placed at this level in the company from outside the medical technology industry.
2. No person of color had held a position at this level.
3. The Mountain Region had been grossly underserved from the corporate level. The representatives in that region had been on their own in many respects and deemed "mavericks." Though their results were respectable, there was a tremendous amount of room for improvement.

You may be thinking that I was being set up for failure. I saw it as the opposite: an opportunity to succeed like never before. This was a leadership challenge I was excited about. Talk about an opportunity for growth!

I was confident in my abilities, and I promised to deliver. The only request I made of the leaders to whom I reported was, "When I ask for support, give it." They agreed. I knew I wouldn't take advantage of that commitment with pointless demands. I committed to deliver my personal best and began the process of doing just that.

Spoiler alert: I wouldn't be writing a book about leadership if my journey into this new and challenging arena wasn't successful. The real value from this experience is that the strategies developed and applied during this time continue to be successful for many other organizations today, including government entities.

This book provides an in-depth look at the myriad steps required to lead a team, division, or an entire organization to top performance. You might be wondering how this book is different from all the others on the topic of leadership. Here are just two ways in which the constructs of this book are different:

1. Because of the necessity to relate to a multi-generational workforce, I provide a different perspective on leadership skills than most when it comes to communicating effectively within an organization.
2. As a result of living in a data-driven world, I will show you what's important to measure as a leader, and why.

My experience in this area has proven invaluable in my own leadership roles *and* to others who constantly strive to rise to new leadership challenges. Let the content in these pages serve you as well as you grow and develop as a leader in today's marketplace.

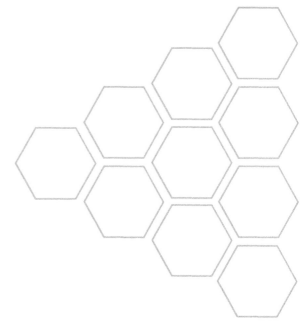

PART 1

ALIGNMENT IS THE RESPONSIBILITY OF LEADERSHIP

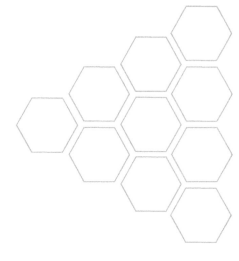

CHAPTER 1

THE ROLE
OF LEADERSHIP IN
ALIGNMENT

"People buy into the leader before they buy into the vision."
– John Maxwell

There are a number of challenges to address when taking on a new leadership role. Perhaps your peers doubt you or, if you've been promoted ahead of them, are jealous of you. Perhaps those you've been assigned to lead have had bad past experiences with previous leaders or have had multiple leaders over a relatively short period of time. It could be a situation where you're coming into the position from outside the industry. There could even be preconceived notions about you due to your gender, race, age, education, or experience that need to be overcome. In fact, those are just a few issues new leaders—as well as experienced leaders taking on new positions—face every day. It comes with the territory. The important thing is to recognize what your specific challenges are and prepare to address them in a direct manner.

No matter your level of experience, coming in with grand plans to make sweeping changes is rarely the answer. You may have a desire, or even an executive order, to achieve drastically improved results, but doing so without first getting the lay of the land is a huge mistake. Getting an accurate picture of where you're starting from requires not only getting to know your direct reports and the culture of the organization, but the data related to current performance.

It should be relatively simple to get the statistics generated by past performance of the individuals on the team from the finance department. Determining *why* they performed at that level and what you can do about improving it is a whole different ballgame. Through the correct analytical processes, leaders can quickly figure out where their organizations stand relative to alignment and what it will take to become more aligned.

Why Alignment Matters

Alignment is defined as being in a position of agreement or an appropriate relative position. According to learning and development leader Steven W. Semler: "Organizational alignment is the degree to which an organization's design, strategy and culture are cooperating to achieve the same desired goals. It is a measurement of the agreement or relative distance between several ideal and real elements of organizational life. Strong alignment requires agreement rather than conflict among the strategic, structural and cultural variables."[1] Alignment occurs when individuals, systems, and processes are operating at optimal performance for the benefit of all an organization's stakeholders—both internal and external.

Measuring employee engagement has been a standard practice in organizations for decades. It was the next evolution after determining levels of employee job satisfaction that began in the 1970s. With measurement of engagement, employers learn not only if their people are satisfied with their jobs and leadership, but whether they really *want* to do their jobs at high levels.

The thought behind engagement is that employees who are engaged in their work will perform better. That makes perfect sense until it is revealed that individuals can be well-engaged but doing the wrong things. With *alignment*, on the other hand, there is a wholehearted match made between employee engagement and the mission and vision of the organization, which leads to an entirely different level of performance results.

When organizations are out of alignment, here's what happens:

1. Individuals are disconnected from the mission and vision.
2. Departments and teams rarely interact with each other. They become closed off to what is considered "outside interference."
3. There's a sense of mistrust of management and a lot of water cooler conversations, which are nothing more than a waste of valuable work time.

4. All or nearly all allotted sick days are taken each year.
5. Turnover is high—often due to burnout.
6. Training budgets are high because new individuals are constantly being onboarded.

On the flip side, when individuals, teams, divisions, and entire organizations operate in alignment, performance levels skyrocket in areas that truly make a difference:

1. Customer satisfaction increases.
2. Turnover is reduced.
3. There are fewer sick days taken.
4. Strategies for improvement come from every direction, not just from the top down.
5. There is a strong sense of purpose exhibited.
6. Individuals readily work across departments, teams, and divisions for the betterment of all.
7. Market share and profitability increase.

Having individuals perform better is a fundamental goal for any organization. However, having them do so while aligned to the common goal or purpose of the organization takes the cumulative effect of high performance to a new level. This higher level benefits the organization, the various individuals working there, *and* the end-user of the products and services produced.

Matching Performance to Purpose

Jack Welch is famous for saying, "Having the best idea doesn't mean you have a winner. You need the best people *aligned to your mission* who are excited every day to deliver results." In a data-driven business environment, working in alignment takes engagement a step further and adds a critical layer of purpose. It's one thing for employees to like their jobs and the people on their teams, which engagement reveals. However, when employees don't have any idea of how their roles connect to the reason the organization exists, they can't see their purpose, and there's a disconnect to the mission and vision. The result is a lower level of performance, especially when challenges arise.

There's a great story about John F. Kennedy that demonstrates this. In 1961, JFK was visiting NASA headquarters after challenging them to put a man on the moon. While touring the facility, he introduced himself to a man in the hallway and asked what he did there. The man explained that he was a janitor. Then, he stated, "I'm helping put a man on the moon!" The janitor recognized that by doing *his* job well, he was contributing to the bigger picture. He was engaged, recognized his purpose, and was aligned to the mission and vision of NASA.

Engagement + Purpose = Alignment

This book is committed to teaching what has been learned through the process of gaining and utilizing the right data to better understand the skills and talents of team members; getting commitment from employees around the company's structure and strategy, and building a culture that enables both the company and its employees to succeed at a higher level of performance through alignment.

Medtronic: Where It All Began

The genesis of this alignment process was through my experience at a company called Medtronic. While Medtronic is the world's largest medical device company, the majority of its sales and profits are generated from the U.S. health care system. Its devices include pacemakers, cardiac rhythm devices, electrosurgical hardware and instruments, cardiac mapping products and monitors, insulin pumps, testing products, and bone-conductive hearing devices. The goal of Medtronic's sales team is to provide quality products that improve patients' lives. The salespeople work directly and in-person with physicians, making recommendations on which products would be in the best therapeutic interests of patients based on the physician's evaluations of their conditions.

As a reminder, I was brought into Medtronic from outside the industry as a diversity hire. In the minds of some, that gave me two strikes before I even got started. Bringing in those without industry experience was a very rare, if not unheard-of, occurrence in the medical device field. It was believed by most insiders that the possibility of achieving success was quite limited if you did not have solid industry experience. And, with those who focused on me as being a diversity hire, my track record of success at a Fortune 500 company meant very little.

I received a fair amount of rejection early on. This rejection came from my peers, who didn't believe I could succeed because of my lack of experience inside the industry, as well as the reps in that region who had been underserved by corporate.

I was the third vice president they'd had in this role in a relatively short period of time.

I had to work hard to be recognized as a strong leader; to work collaboratively with my peers, empower my team to be accountable to the company's mission and vision, and encourage creativity, career development, and best practices.

My specific position was that of vice president of sales for the flagship products of pacemakers and cardiac rhythm devices in the Mountain Region. This was an expansive part of the country, with representatives working in areas from Albuquerque to Anchorage. In between this territory was some rough terrain, much of which the sales team had not previously traveled, due largely to the time constraints in traveling such distances. Many hospital leaders and physicians in this region had not seen Medtronic representatives for years and were not happy about the lack of attention. Much of the business that was going to the competition was simply because they showed up, and we didn't.

In studying the competition, it was obvious that they were more clearly aligned. They had more products. They covered the territory better. Physicians were up to speed on their products. Patients were asking for those products. More profit was being generated. While hospital administrators wanted medical device products on their shelves, they had not seen a Medtronic executive in a very long time.

Interestingly, when physicians were asked which device brand they would recommend for their own parents, 85 percent said they'd want Medtronic devices. However, Medtronic only had 55 percent market share. This disparity clearly showed a lot of opportunity.

With Medtronic's headquarters in Minneapolis, the Mountain Region was as far removed from the company's thinking as it was in miles. The sales team in the Mountain Region had been under-served in both the level of attention given to their needs and by lack of direct, personal contact from leadership. Most had established their own ways of doing business. And, as their new leader, I was initially perceived as a potential threat to the status quo.

As for me, I quickly understood what I was up against. To say I had a lot to learn was a gross understatement, but I was prepared to bring my best to the challenge. I was fortunate to have a strong group of first-line managers in the Mountain Region. Because of their isolation and interrupted leadership, they had a lot of responsibility. Understanding that they would be skeptical of me for the many reasons mentioned above, I had to approach them carefully. One of my direct reports, Bob Mohle, remembers that I came in with an upbeat attitude and a desire to learn—rather than arriving ready to lay down the law as the new sheriff in town. I didn't run from the fact that I came from outside the industry, or that I had never lived in that region of the country. I simply explained my strengths as a leader and belief in the team's ability to achieve a higher level of performance.

The bottom line about medical technology companies is that their products save lives. What few outsiders understand is that those products have highly complex components within them. Representatives don't just make a sale, drop off equipment, and move on to the next client. They educate physicians. They consult on patient evaluations. They are present in the catheterization lab when physicians implant the devices. They test and adjust the devices for the best results for each patient. They are on call for the doctors, and their schedules are not their own.

Furthermore, physicians are not loyal. If the rep had a conflict in their schedule that precluded them from being present when the doctor needed him, it was highly likely the doctor would switch to the competition's product. Because of this, maintaining business could be tougher than getting new customers. It's not uncommon for medical device reps to work 70-hour weeks supporting their clients: both the physicians and hospitals. Operating at that level of commitment for any length of time requires a sense of greater purpose. Otherwise, reps burn out quickly.

While I was confident in my ability to grow business because of my previous experience, it was critical to gain industry and product knowledge as quickly as possible. I attended tech training, studied the competition, and became very familiar with Medtronic's history.

One of the unique facets of Medtronic is that it is a mission-driven company. In other words, it's a company that pursues sales not just for the sake of profitability, but more importantly, for the benefit of the patients helped by its products. Because of the life-enriching importance of Medtronic's products, and the need for these products to perform well, everyone at the company—from design engineers to product assembly technicians to salespeople to executives—needed to be aligned around the company's mission.

Part of the onboarding process for every new hire is what I affectionately call a "brainwashing session," which was intended to share Medtronic's origin and mission. This process includes meeting the company's founder (which was Earl Bakken when he was alive) or the most senior executive who then talked about the company's origins, how it has evolved, and what the business means to the patients.

The goal of this session is to sear the information into the hearts and minds of employees, so they do not lose sight of what they are working for. As with most large corporations, the leaders at Medtronic believe this onboarding ceremony is critical to getting full buy-in from the employee base. It works well to a certain degree—at least when you first come on board with the company as an excited new hire. The problem that became obvious to me was that the initial excitement didn't last.

I soon discovered that the further employees were physically removed from the company's headquarters, the more disconnected they became from the company's mission and vision. For whatever reason, outside of having employees understand the company's mission during onboarding, leaders in the company didn't make the effort to connect that mission with plans, processes, and actions.

Discovering the Real Problems

Quickly recognizing a disconnect between engagement and performance, I asked the people in Medtronic's human resources department, "What do we use to measure the alignment of our employees with the company's mission?" The reply was, "We measure engagement every year."

I understood engagement studies. However, based on the results we were getting, I was concerned that we were measuring the wrong things. *Engagement* is the extent to which employees feel valued and involved in their work. That was all well and good, but I needed to know *why* they felt that way, then drill down into each of the categories of alignment to determine what could be done to convert those "feelings" into higher performance.

Not finding an instrument to measure alignment, I decided to put together my own and connect with others for assistance. I reached out to a handful of PhDs in organizational effectiveness and organizational development, some human resource executives, and professionals, and those in the field of educational psychology from reputable universities for help. We determined there were nine pillars that needed to be evaluated. Initially, we came up with a survey instrument that was 100 questions long. While we felt those questions would generate useful data, we feared those taking it would end up with what is known as "survey fatigue." With too many questions to answer, those taking the surveys are likely to lose interest and fail to provide accurate answers. So, we went back to the drawing board. After about a year, we reduced the number of questions to 21. At that point, I was confident we could push this instrument out to the organization and get the data we needed. The primary purpose was to define areas of disconnect that we could work to improve.

The initial response from the managers, sales reps, and clinical support people was, of course, "Oh, *another* survey?" To get buy-in from them to respond accurately, it was communicated that the survey was a way for them to have an impact on the organization. They were invited to let their voices resonate with leadership. This was the beginning of an extremely valuable two-way communication.

Once the data was assembled, I pulled my leadership team together to review the information and come up with suggestions to address the problems it revealed. As they dove into the information, I noted an increased energy in the room. Everyone was on board with wanting to improve the team's performance.

What the data revealed about the lack of alignment was clear, and we were able to design a strategic plan to address each issue. (We'll go over each issue and how it was resolved later in the book.) Each individual took on specific action items aligned to the company mission and vision. We got leadership buy-in to 360-degree accountability for these plans and put measures in place to get buy-in from everyone else who would be involved. We developed feedback loops for communication, linkages between leadership and the team members, and created opportunities for increased teamwork.

About eight months later, we measured our progress and had everyone retake the assessment. We were able to substantially improve performance across the entire region through increased coherence and connectivity within the leadership that was then driven down the organization. Another of my direct reports, Larry Saunders, appreciated the "outside the box" approach we took from an organizational standpoint. He recognized that the sense of empowerment and trust within the region was transformational. Ingrid Torres, in human resources at Medtronic, acknowledged the tremendous change in the managers—especially long-term managers—when the new plans were implemented. She saw more ownership taken by district managers. There was more enthusiasm for developing solutions and owning outcomes than ever before.

Our initial alignment scores showed that we were pretty average, which is referred to as being "semi-aligned." After implementing the new strategic plans and providing effective feedback loops for the team, we were able to raise our scores to indicate that we were "strongly aligned," and greater performance in the entire region was the result.

Everyone was on board and took these new plans seriously. They recognized how much better we were getting in communicating, acquiring market share, and increasing revenue. We all saw how much our work was impacting the bottom line, and how many more customers were being served—and served well.

The outcome of that work was that we were able to grow top-line revenue by 13% year-over-year in a flat market. Considering that we were a market leader at 55% of market share, that was an incredibly difficult thing to do! Yet, once we were able to focus on the real problems at hand, it became doable. All of this contributed to building an exceptional team that had the highest level of compounded annual growth rate during my five years in that role. Our data supported the fact that the more aligned an organization is to its mission and vision, the better it performs.

I believe that with the right data, any leader can accomplish similar results and be able to transform an organization from one that's "going through the motions" to one in which people see the purpose of their work and perform—doing the right things—at their highest level. In other words, with the right data, individual performance can be greatly improved by getting the organization in alignment. That's because the environment is then consistent with who they are and what they believe to be true. They *want* to be a part of it!

The Art of Alignment

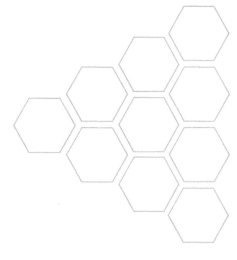

CHAPTER 2

CHANGING PERSPECTIVE

*"We cannot solve today's problems with the same
thinking used when we created them."*
– Albert Einstein

Before any roadmap or strategic plan can be developed to improve performance and revenue, it's essential to determine where you're starting from. This requires an evaluation of the current level of performance of your team or organization. Once the current information shows "where you are," a more in-depth analysis can be considered as to why the results are what they are. Leaders must look at the actions that are currently being taken from a variety of perspectives and ask questions that lead to new (and better) alternatives. But first, we must ask this question: How aligned is my team or organization? To understand how to evaluate the answer to that question, let's consider the various levels of alignment.

Levels of Alignment

For simplicity's sake, alignment scores are divided into three types:

1. **Misaligned**: Organizations that score below 35% on alignment assessments.
2. **Semi-aligned**: Organizations that score in a range of 35% to 64%.
3. **Strongly aligned**: Organizations that typically score 65% and above.

It's important to note that due to the myriad of parts contributing to alignment within an organization, it would be impossible to achieve a 100% alignment score. The difference in even a small percentage of alignment can be massive in the performance of a team or organization and the level of results achieved.

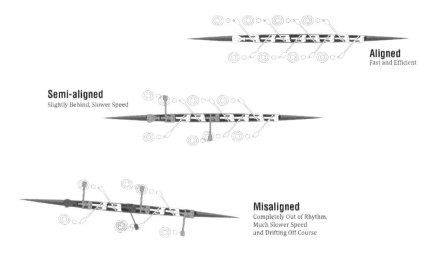

Aligned
Fast and Efficient

Semi-aligned
Slightly Behind, Slower Speed

Misaligned
Completely Out of Rhythm,
Much Slower Speed
and Drifting Off Course

The most prominent missing element in **misaligned** teams is how they relate to the mission of the organization. While the mission and purpose of the organization may be delivered to employees upon hiring, strategic plans and goals are not linked back to that mission and vision. Few individuals will see how their roles and actions directly impact the organization's mission and vision. They simply go to work and do their jobs with little thought about the bigger picture. While employees may be diligent in doing their individual jobs, the organization, as a whole, lacks a sense of shared purpose and accountability.

In the misaligned organization, the whole is never greater than the sum of its parts. For a quick indicator of how aligned your organization is, ask a few individuals if they can recite the mission statement. More importantly, can *you* recite the mission with 100 percent accuracy? If not, the work to be done begins with you.

Most organizations fall into the category of being **semi-aligned**. This type of organization is fairly solid. In fact, its engagement scores may be quite good. It does fairly well in its marketplaces despite its lack of strong alignment. However, it is often inconsistent or lacking sustainability. These organizations can marshal forces around a strategic goal for a period of time, but that higher level of performance just doesn't last.

The overall mission and vision of semi-aligned organizations are only occasionally included in messages throughout the company or used to guide decisions. Few on the team truly get behind the message being delivered by the leaders. They just don't see the direction the company is going or believe management is providing sufficient support for a continued high level of performance.

Strongly aligned organizations have a mission and purpose that is shared repeatedly and understood across teams, departments, and divisions, and their actions are driven by that understanding. The mission and vision are meaningful to all employees and allow them to connect to something bigger than themselves.

The mission guides decision-making at all levels. It helps everyone see the connections between individual performance, strategic plans, and performance goals. The mission puts context around the organization's purpose, which reduces turnover and may attract high performers. Leaders are accessible, candid, and authentic throughout consistent communications with each other and their teams. There is a strong sense of accountability, and there is collaboration across teams.

Once your organization's level of alignment is determined, the job of leadership is not to charge ahead with new ideas and strategies to improve performance. Instead, the responsibility of leadership is to consider why the data is what it is, ask questions related to current methods and levels of communication, and then look at things through a different set of lenses.

Look Through Different Lenses

Moving teams and organizations that have stagnated or have poor or average alignment toward higher performance requires leaders to consider different points of view. In some cases, this will begin with leaders asking themselves questions about their own performance if it is not where they want it to be. Strong leaders do not hesitate to start with themselves and what they could be doing differently to drive or encourage improved results.

Before any new actions can be taken within divisions or teams, the leadership of the organization must discover the challenge areas, get 360-degree feedback on those areas, and then develop strategic plans to increase performance. While doing this, it's important to consider that the current challenges might be due to having flawed strategic plans. They also might be due to the culture of the organization, or even the perception of leadership by individuals.

Before discovering different solutions to problems, leaders must view their current situations through different lenses or from different perspectives. There are four key lenses that can make all the difference in the level of alignment within an organization.

They are:

1. Leadership transparency
2. Flying in formation
3. Doing things differently
4. Winning over hearts and minds

Leaders of misaligned or semi-aligned organizations might initially balk at viewing their organizations through these four lenses. That's normal. Change is not easy for everyone. However, those who have a strong desire to improve performance and reap the results because of their passion for their organizations will take whatever positive steps are necessary to get the job done. Now, let's dive deep into the four lenses through which to view your organization.

Lens #1: Leadership Transparency

Leaders need to help the people they lead to know, like, and trust them. It's essential that leaders share who they are and what they stand for. Being an open book when it comes to personal background, the experience the leader brings to the role, and their passion for excellence will go far. Organizations move at the speed of trust, and trust is dependent upon predictability. When leaders are predictable, individuals are more inclined to stay focused on their part of the plan rather than being distracted by fear, gossip, and speculation.

Leaders of aligned organizations need to let the team members see their human sides. Great leaders cannot just be names on the organizational chart of the company. This does not mean that leaders should necessarily become "chummy" with team members. Doing so quickly opens the doors to questions about favoritism. Rather, the goal is to help team members understand four things about their leaders:

1. Who they are
2. Where they come from/what they have done
3. Their intentions as the leaders of the team
4. Their belief in where the team can go *together*

It's one thing for leaders to get people to like them. It requires additional proof of their abilities to lead in order to get those team members to adhere to viable strategic plans.

> Shortly after taking on the role of regional leader, I invited my team of direct reports at Medtronic to play a round of golf and then come to my home for dinner. In doing so, I shared with them, quite literally, who I was. They met my wife and kids. They were welcome to walk around the house. The floor was open for them to ask questions about my life and what drove me to succeed as their leader.
>
> The Johnson clan hails from a small town in Mississippi. On my wall, there is a picture of a document that shows the assets of the plantation where my family resided. This document reflects the number of chickens and pigs and has a list of slaves. My great-great-grandfather Philmore is listed on this document as property. When I shared this with the team, it was not hard for them to understand my family background.
>
> My team also saw evidence of my personal background as a participant in high school and collegiate sports. This helped them see that I had team experience. I hoped it would demonstrate to them that I would be steadfast in my efforts to be a part of *their* team.

This invitation to get to know me provided clarity in terms of what it is that I am about, where I come from, and that I have nothing to hide. I am who I profess to be: someone with a humble family history; someone who has succeeded in a team environment; someone with a passion for improving my own performance as well as that of the team.

The combination of my family history and personal background helped my team bond with me and encouraged them to let their guard down. Their minds became open to the strategic plan I had presented to increase revenue in the region. And, most importantly, they felt comfortable providing unadulterated feedback on that plan. Their feedback provided tremendous insight into how well the plan might work and my own part in driving its implementation. It was the beginning of the development of a meaningful working relationship.

Through the use of this first lens, I saw a massive change in perspective among my team members from, "Hey, wait a minute. I don't really know this person the organization is telling me I must follow" to "You know what? I can get behind this guy as a leader because I understand his life experiences and believe he will follow through." This get-together went a long way toward establishing trust.

The goal of this first lens is to provide each team member an opportunity to truly understand the leader. As tech executive and billionaire Sheryl Sandberg states in her lectures, "True leadership stems from individuality that is honestly and sometimes imperfectly expressed ... leaders should strive for authenticity over perfection." It's essential that leaders demonstrate humility, admitting they're not perfect and that accomplishing the plan requires everyone to bring their individual expertise to its implementation. This is also when leaders encourage two-way communication.

When you invest time and effort in getting to know others, it shows that you care. There's a well-known truism that has been attributed to everyone from Theodore Roosevelt to John Maxwell: "People won't care how much you know until they know how much you care." Understanding leads to trust and respect. This includes respect for leaders, fellow team members, and the goal everyone is expected to accomplish together. Once trust is built, there is a foundation of support for the leader, the collaborative planning efforts, and, most importantly, for the execution of plans.

As individuals let down their guards, they will offer genuine feedback. In this type of culture, as trust mitigates the fear of reprisal, there is more calculated risk-taking, which often leads to more favorable outcomes. Once leaders receive the right input, they can take the steps necessary to get the right output from the team. That's how you create a meaningful working relationship between leaders and teams.

Lens #2: Flying in Formation

Formation flying is the disciplined flight of two or more aircraft under the command of a flight leader. In the military, formations are used to concentrate firepower and create a mutual defense. This method of flight was designed after studying migratory birds that fly in a V formation, such as Canadian geese. Their wingtips are carefully positioned and synchronized to catch the preceding bird's updraft and save energy during flight. This is an excellent analogy for leaders to share when seeking to gain commitment from teams to perform at higher levels. You're not asking individuals for gargantuan efforts; you are asking for and helping them understand that getting into alignment concentrates effort and yields significant performance results.

One of the greatest advantages of flying in formation is to avoid burnout. Flying out of formation creates challenges and stress within the organization—it's a distraction that takes everyone's eyes off the prize. Getting into that sweet spot of moving forward in formation benefits everyone on the team.

To achieve this type of team commitment, it is necessary to establish a clear understanding of the roles and responsibilities required to execute a strategic plan. Depending on the nature of the organization, formations might need to be dynamic, flexing with the demands of the marketplace or developments in the industry. The degree to which everyone understands the roles and expectations—and commits to their fulfillment by doing their jobs well—increases the likelihood of overall success.

Due to the nature of the work an individual does, their position in the formation may flux according to the strategic plan, even though their job description does not. In some cases, their skills and talents may come to the forefront. In other cases, their amount of involvement may be minimal. In either case, a high level of performance is what is needed, and the change in their roles may need to be addressed to increase their understanding of what is expected of them and why.

To use some sports metaphors, it's imperative to help individuals understand that not everyone is going to shoot the ball. Not everyone is going to catch the touchdown pass. Not everyone is going to receive the puck in a spot where they can score.

Yet, each member of the team has a responsibility in terms of ensuring success. The degree to which everyone understands what those roles and expectations are increases the likelihood of organizational success.

Unfortunately, there will be people whose opinions and actions range from having no interest in flying in formation to outright opposition to doing so. Data and experience indicate that whenever a new plan is introduced, only about one-fourth of those involved will fully engage and be committed. Half of the team will waffle, and the last one-fourth will likely be dissenters. Leaders should not be surprised by these numbers, nor should they allow them to negatively impact the implementation of the strategy. When putting together a new initiative, allow time for dealing with those who do not get on board right away. This is simply a typical challenge of leadership.

Rather than working directly with the dissenters, a leadership position may require working with lower-level leaders or managers to help them ask the right questions and then feed the information back up the line. Doing so empowers those lower-level leaders and managers and reinforces their own buy-in to the plans.

When leaders face dissension, it may be necessary to sort out the dissenters individually and communicate directly with them. The wafflers will eventually settle on one side or the other, while the out-and-out dissenters may need a more direct course of action.

Wise leaders go straight to the source of the dissension. However, they don't charge in. They express a desire to listen first, then act. They ask open-ended questions and take notes on the input received. They make it known that the dissenters' voices are being heard and their concerns duly noted.

Rather than reacting to the dissension or attempting to overcome the challenges presented during communication with dissenters, wise leaders ask for time to consider the information provided. Then, they establish a time frame to respond. As the leader, you are trying to change the culture of dissension, and that takes time. Asking for time to get back to dissenters empowers them and obligates you—even if you're not going to make any changes to the plan based on the information provided. Most dissenters will simply be happy to have been heard. For the rest of them, once the issues have been addressed one way or the other, most will appreciate having been heard and be more likely to support future initiatives because of it.

When a new initiative is introduced and people disagree with it, it's critical to remain open-minded. As a leader, you must invest the time to understand why people are not initially supporting it. There may be a cultural issue that needs to be addressed on a broader level. There could be a structural issue that stands in the way of success. Perhaps there is something fundamentally wrong with the plan that you and your peers have not recognized.

When dissenters are not given the opportunity to be listened to, they will likely work against the plan behind the scenes or sow negative discord. This happens through sidebar conversations, dragging their feet on implementation or ignoring the initiative altogether. It's better to directly address dissenters as soon as possible to keep them from distracting the rest of the team or cannonballing the entire plan.

There will be times when the dissension is among the ranks of leadership. Strong leaders are able to demonstrate how to constructively challenge other leaders in a respectful way and foster open dialogue. When a high-level leader says something averse to what a lower leader understands, there needs to be an opportunity for open dialogue around that utterance.

Let's say that a top leader says, "We need to increase market share while keeping our prices the same." That could be construed as a conflicting message if past increases in market share were obtained through discounting. Rather than directly pointing out the flaw in this thinking, it might be wise to ask for suggestions from both fellow and upline leaders as to how this might be implemented. Demonstrate support for the idea so as not to be deemed a dissenter, but still ask questions. To enlighten the leader of the challenge, you might ask if one aspect is more important than the other (because you don't see how to achieve both).

Not all dissenters will feel comfortable sharing their concerns with those in leadership positions. It's up to the leader to provide a venue in which others feel comfortable about expressing themselves. In some cases, a survey of the dissenters might be necessary. In other cases, some small group or one-on-one conversations will be all it takes to resolve matters.

Depending on the leader's relationship with the dissenters, getting them to open up might require meeting for an off-site coffee, sharing a meal, or grabbing a beer in a relaxed environment.

Wise leaders will ask questions similar to these:

- "If you were going to do this differently, how would you do it?"
- "If you could change anything in this plan, what would you change?"

It falls to the leader to create that level of conversation so people will be more likely to open up and fully express themselves, and then to actively listen to the answers.

It could be that the dissenters simply didn't understand the initiative due to the way the leader communicated it. Once it's known *why* people are in disagreement, it can then be determined *how* to proceed with creating the alignment necessary for success. Remember, people who contribute to a plan are more likely to buy into it. When dissension leads to clarity, those who previously fought the plan may become its biggest advocates.

There will always be those who will not go along with the necessary changes for everyone to "fly in formation." Because of this, some tough decisions may have to be made, including giving people opportunities to find employment elsewhere. With some dissenters, it may be discovered that they would benefit the initiative better in a different role within the company. Whatever the case, each situation needs to be weighed on its own merit.

Experience has shown that some direct reports or managers may operate better as individual contributors. With the introduction of a new plan, it may become obvious that they just don't have it in them to cascade messages of support throughout their teams. However, they may have other skillsets that could prove valuable to the execution.

Trust and Predictability Are Synonymous

If someone is unpredictable, you can't trust them. It's as simple as that. To the degree that what someone is going to do can be predicted—even if it's bad—they can be trusted to do it. It's vital to note the contrast between trust and common moral values, as they are two very different things. Many people misconstrue trust and moral compass. Their thinking tends to be, "If someone does something I wouldn't do, I can't trust them." That's simply not true. The ideal, of course, would be to work with people who are predictable *and* have the same moral principles. Alignment between those who are alike in both can happen in a moment. Alignment between those who are predictable and have different moral principles takes extra effort. However, when leaders can predict how someone will act or react in a business situation, there is trust.

For those people who have valuable skill sets, leadership may have to set up a handicap and formulate plans around them. If doing so is too cumbersome or might negatively impact other aspects of the strategic plan, decisions might need to be made to move that person either to another position within the organization or to the outside.

Wise leaders never assume that all the players are in the right positions on the team or should stay in the same positions when strategic plans change. Leaders are always on the lookout for ways to rearrange the players for the benefit of the organization as a whole—not so much to be disruptive, but to improve. People who stay in a given role too long are likely to exhibit cronyism, which leads to stagnation and a decrease in morale within the team.

Each industry is different. If strategic plans are changing to address market dynamics at a fast rate, it may become necessary to generate some turnover in leadership positions rather than keeping someone who may be married to the last plan and slow to adapt. There can be a delicate balance between leadership turnover and cronyism. For industries with slower market changes, it may be just fine to keep people in place for longer terms.

Remember: When change is necessary, the longer you take to make a leadership change, the more you're hurting the organization. Individuals will recognize when this happens. And when deficiencies are seen within the leadership and nothing happens to improve the situation, credibility diminishes.

Recognition Programs

Once clear expectations are understood at the individual level, it's important to set up recognition programs to reflect the work that's going on. Business advisor Sharon Lechter teaches in her lectures, "A person who is appreciated will always do more than expected." Recognizing positive actions starts with catching people doing the right thing in coordination with the mission and vision and rewarding those actions. Doing so sets up a reverberation effect among the individuals. They begin to feel the following:

- "I committed to the plan."
- "I completed my role and responsibilities to the best of my ability."
- "I'm excited about my role in the success of the plan."
- "My part in the plan was recognized."

When you create that effect, individuals will feel compelled to "rinse and repeat" many times over, doing their share to keep the organization in alignment and performing at its highest level.

> When we had a banner year in the Mountain Region of Medtronic, I wanted to reward my direct reports in a big way. There had been a lot expected of them. There were many times when we were wringing our hands over how to achieve the high-level goals we had chosen. I felt it was necessary to reward not only those on my team, but to do so in front of the spouses and significant others who had supported the gargantuan effort put forth.
>
> That effort was memorialized at a recognition event. Each member of my team received a Tag Heuer watch inscribed with a message about the accomplishment. To make this a long-lasting recognition and further stamp the significance of the work, I hand-wrote a letter to each of their parents, acknowledging their child's work and how it would impact our patients.

Lens #3: Doing Things Differently

"Doing things differently" is another take on the adage about doing the same things yet expecting a different result. To gain market share, organizations must continuously change and adapt, even when they are the market leaders. Some potential clients will have strong relationships with the competition. To win them over, organizations need to stand out from the crowd.

Too many companies look only at what the competition is doing and focus on doing the same thing—only better. The thinking is that, "If we do it better, we will take those clients for ourselves." Wise leaders understand that doing the same thing as the competition may not be what's needed. They are open to seeking valuable approaches from multiple sources, including outside their industries.

The same issue may have been faced by organizations in entirely different fields. Insights could be found in non-business organizations, in nature, watching children interact with each other, or even within the potential client's organization itself. Transformational leaders are typically curious learners who actively develop their perceptive capabilities. They seek ideas from other sources that have successfully dealt with any issue they're working on—no matter the industry.

As an example, Medtronic primarily conducted business through hospitals to physicians. The physicians would then recommend the products to the patients. This put Medtronic in a position of being twice removed from the end-user. Doing things differently became critical in articulating the value proposition of both the product and service to the patients. This was done in ways that would be acceptable in the eyes of the patients, yet not step on the toes of the doctors.

Messaging about the Medtronic mission and vision was created for distribution through social media and advertising directly to potential patients (not unlike recent pharmaceutical advertising). Medtronic's mission was to alleviate pain, restore health, and extend life. When the patients understood the *benefits* of the products, it was easier to generate new business as they asked their physicians about them. This messaging caused less resistance to Medtronic products and services.

Lens #4: Winning Over Hearts and Minds

Once you have everyone in both leadership and management positions committed to driving the plan throughout the organization, it's time to win over the hearts and minds of the broader employee base. This has to be done with an appreciation for employees' roles, responsibilities, and perspectives.

People will find it hard to get on board with you, your ideologies, or your plan unless they feel you understand where they're coming from. You have to not only understand their positions on the plan, but also articulate them and, even more importantly, empathize with them. It's one thing to have a group of leaders who have great empathy; it's another when they can express it in a manner that drives the behavior they're looking for from the staff.

Leaders at all levels must understand how to be clear in their recognition of the contribution of individuals in a manner that sears the strategic plan into the hearts and minds of all. At the same time, leaders must show the direct correlation between that plan and the mission of the organization. One way to do this is to share the stories of the end-users of your products. Capturing these stories and delivering them in the best manner may require road trips to some obscure areas. It may require visiting satellite offices with only a few employees. It may require arranging to meet actual end-users in person, shaking their hands, and listening to their stories. Once learned, it becomes crucial to share those stories within the organization and tie them back to the corporate mission and vision. When leadership operates at such a level, it sends a cohesive, positive message throughout the organization and establishes a culture of caring.

There was a sales representative for Medtronic who hadn't taken a vacation day in years. She had an expansive territory of 100 miles in all directions. Her days began at 5 a.m. and often ended at 10 p.m. She missed many activities in her children's lives and many events with extended family and friends. There was a culture in the company at that time that suggested that if you took even one day off, it was an invitation for the competition to come in and try to steal your clients.

I visited her region to thank her personally for her work ethic and for living the corporate mission. I showed her that I understood the sacrifices she was making and shared the stories of patients whose lives had been dramatically changed for the better through her efforts.

Her heart and mind were on fire with passion for the mission and vision of Medtronic! Her commitment was rewarded with some well-deserved time off and a promotion. She was also invited to participate in a task force to address the problem of employee burnout due to a lack of life/work balance. Because of her experience and her passion for the company mission and vision, she was able to put a plan together that helped resolve this issue for herself (and others) that is still in place today.

To win the hearts and minds of others, it's critical for leaders to express understanding and appreciation of the efforts of those who are going above and beyond toward the achievement of the mission. This appreciation should always be tied back to how the end consumer benefits. The formula is this:

**Recognize > Empathize >
Tie to strategic plan and mission**

Recognize the work that has been done. Empathize with the complexity of the work. Tie the effort, intention and outcome to the strategic plan and mission. Then rinse and repeat with consistency. That's how effective leaders win over the hearts and minds of the individuals within teams or entire organizations.

Different perspectives often bring new opportunities to light. By viewing your organization through the four lenses, adjustments can be made to strategic plans or to how they are presented. New actions can be taken, and a deeper level of commitment can be generated. All of this leads to greater alignment with the mission and vision, which leads to greater performance.

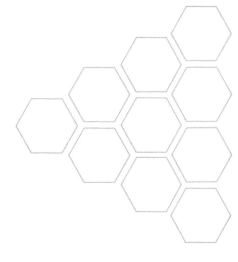

CHAPTER 3

ANYONE CAN BE
A GREAT LEADER

"Leadership is an action, not a position."
– Donald McGannon

There is no such thing as a natural-born leader. However, anyone can become a great leader when they're willing to pay the price. Leadership skills are gained through experience and then honed by challenges. Leaders develop winning attitudes and even temperaments and are willing to grow and develop their skills for the advancement of the organization and the advantages that winning brings. They learn about mission and vision and alignment and how to pull it all together for the benefit of everyone involved. This means putting the organization and its team first.

I was fortunate to learn a lot about leadership from my father. In his early life, he was a skinny, dyslexic D student who rose to the position of Chairman of the Board of Directors of the Federal Reserve Bank of Minneapolis. His fundamental beliefs about leadership were as follows:

1. Treat everyone with respect.
2. Remove all impediments to progress quickly.
3. Ask provocative questions and LISTEN!
4. Lead by example.
5. Surround yourself with talent that makes you better and drives performance.
6. Sell the vision. Make sure everyone knows the role they play and how it contributes to the goal.
7. Have faith and humility. Always believe in something bigger than you.

These beliefs served him well, catapulting him to leadership roles in everything he did, including becoming the Chairman of the Council of Chairmen, reporting directly to then-Federal Reserve Chairman Alan Greenspan.

When leadership skills are combined with an understanding of people and a desire to succeed, it's possible to get a group of "B-players" to out-perform "A-players." In the early 1990s, UNLV's basketball team consisted of A-players. They outshone the rest of the NCAA all season long. When it came down to the finals, they went up against Duke and were expected to take the championship. Unfortunately, they did not succeed. In the final analysis, the reason UNLV was defeated was that those A-players played an *individual* game. In contrast, Duke played a *team* game with everyone contributing to the end result—not focusing on who got the individual shots.

While A-players may shine with an array of skillsets, they may have a tendency to be prima donnas. When they don't get the big opportunities, they can get frustrated and do things that end up sabotaging the team's success. B-players may only be good at doing one thing, but they're excellent at that one thing and work for the team's benefit. Great leaders identify the skillsets of individuals and, through effective leadership, help them understand their roles and responsibilities. The leader's job then becomes one of aligning the players in such a way that the whole is greater than the sum of its parts.

> My high school basketball coach understood and practiced alignment. When we were going up against a team with a bunch of A-players, he would have us run "Mustang." This strategy was that everyone touched the ball twice before anyone would shoot. This strategy helped us to tire out the members of the opposing team, give them fewer possessions of the ball, and create frustration. Those frustrated players would make wild shots just to get one in. During timeouts, we would see them arguing among themselves, which caused them to lose focus on the big picture of winning the game.
>
> Many times, it's easier to get a B-player in alignment with the team goals than it is to get the A-players to their individual spotlights.

The goal is to bring people into the organization who buy into the ideology of winning as a team. Some of this is done in the vetting process before bringing them on.

A great example of this is with NBA star Dennis Rodman. Early in his career with the Detroit Pistons, he was considered a B-player. He did not make the starting lineup and was instead relegated to the bench. His strength was in his defensive moves and ability to rebound the ball. When he was traded to the Chicago Bulls, his strengths proved to be the perfect match for the shooting skills of Michael Jordan. Through the leadership of coach Phil Jackson, the Bulls placed the right players in the right positions for the team to "fly in formation" and out-performed the rest of the NBA.

For his part, Rodman was given the role and responsibility to do what he did best. Because he knew his role, was dedicated to the mission and vision of the team, and performed his responsibilities to the best of his ability, he developed into an A-player. In fact, he was "one of the best rebounding forwards in NBA history," according to NBA.com. His contribution to the "three-peat" championships of the Chicago Bulls is the stuff of legend.

Getting Everyone Aligned

How is this level of success possible in the corporate world? It's done by first getting everyone on the team aligned around the organization's mission and vision—the goal. This is done through effective communication of the plan. Creating alignment will increase performance across the board, generate greater results, and has been proven to provide a competitive advantage in the marketplace. With a well-developed and well-delivered strategic plan that is tied to the mission and vision of the organization, this advantage can be accomplished within a six-month time period. It's not easy, but it is doable.

Strong leaders, once they've discovered the current challenges within their organizations, harness their skills to implement strategic plans this way:

1. Establishing a common goal. This applies to any arena, whether it's setting a goal to win the Super Bowl or gaining a specific percentage of market share.
2. Making it clear to individuals what their roles are relative to that goal.
3. Making sure that each person's purpose, relative to what they're being asked to do, is congruent with their internal beliefs. Beliefs drive actions, and strong leaders are attuned to the beliefs of their direct reports. They encourage those direct reports to do the same with those they lead.
4. Recognizing progress along the way. This recognition is timely and purposeful. For some, well-received recognition might be in the form of verbal praise and a handshake or hug. For others, a financial reward is what does the trick.

The responsibility for accomplishing those four steps falls on the leaders. Effective leaders will get buy-in from their direct reports through these steps, and those direct reports will drive the same message down the line. Establishing a strategic plan for alignment is a leadership function, but executing it effectively requires the entire team. Leaders are the ones who must anticipate and remove the rocks in the road to achieve the desired end result.

There are some key elements that are involved in effectively recognizing progress by the members of your team.

1. The work required by the plan was done.
2. That work was done well.
3. The work led to positive performance, which equaled positive results.

When leaders are conscious of and act in accordance with those three tenets, they do their jobs well. The definition of **management** is getting work done through others. It is task-driven. **Leadership**, on the other hand, is getting others to do the right things even when leaders are not around, and *especially* when no one is watching.

Leadership involves keeping everyone moving forward on the same mission, even when the wind is blowing in their faces, and it is an uphill battle. This doesn't just involve *what* needs to be accomplished, but also the *purpose* of what the organization is trying to accomplish. The goal of the leader is to make the strategic plan easy to understand and implement. It is critical that individual contributors can grab hold of it and decide the degree to which it is a part of *their* purpose. The closer these two are aligned, the more each employee will lean in, bringing their best selves to their work.

A great example of a leader who is able to do this is basketball coach Mike Krzyzewski of Duke University—known as "Coach K." He has led the Blue Devils to 5 National Collegiate Athletic Association Championships, 12 Final Fours, 12 Atlantic Coast Conference (ACC) regular-season titles, and 15 ACC Tournament championships.

Coach K knows the background of each player before recruiting them. He learns of their experiences—what has shaped their beliefs—before placing them on the team. Krzyzewski is able to articulate what the organization is trying to do in ways that each player will understand and get behind. He is able to look into the eyes of the players and decide which ones are able to carry out the mission and vision. In doing so, he is able to ascertain the degree to which his players have fully bought in to the goal. In other words, the purpose of the broader organization has become *their* purpose.

You can see this dynamic during timeouts when Krzyzewski is addressing the team. You can see the expressions on the faces of those young men—*commitment*. You can almost hear them say, "Not only have I bought in, but I am prepared to go out and execute on what you have defined as necessary to achieve the goal."

If we think about the importance of a leader in any business organization, the leader should not only have the best interests of the organization at heart, but of all the parties involved. The leader must invest the time necessary to establish the roles of each team player. Leaders must be able to communicate how company goals are impacted by the efforts of individuals. They must also be prepared to recognize individuals as they each contribute to the broader cause and provide feedback to them along the way.

Having an engaged level of oversight is critical to leadership success. When recognition and feedback are consistently provided, individuals on the team know when they're moving the needle forward or have the opportunity to make corrections in their actions or activities. Team members get to know that their work is appreciated as it contributes to the purpose of the organization.

The best leaders are effective at doing all these things, which then build to a crescendo of a higher level of performance. Any leader can do that by following the four steps listed above.

Sadly, in many organizations, there is often a group of A-players who cannot "get on the same page" with the rest of the organization. They each operate somewhat in isolation from the team and the overall company. These people are often called "mavericks." Their lack of alignment with the rest of the team can stunt the growth of the entire organization. This is how a group of B-players who are well-led and aligned can out-perform the A-players. It is up to the leader to figure out what the "page" is and how to get buy-in.

How Leaders Develop Strategic Plans

One simple way to begin developing a strategic plan that will lead to alignment is with the organization's financial statements and annual reports. This is where the company expresses and showcases its mission and greater purpose—the focal point of every great plan.

Listen to what is talked about during the shareholders' meetings. This is when and where the organization's vision is shared. Hearing the stories being told and understanding the direction of the larger organization is incredibly valuable to every leader. What direction is the company going? How will they deliver on their mission? When you tie that information to the strategic plan, you create a situation where anyone who goes along with the plan also goes along with the company.

As a leader, you either get buy-in from your employees or you don't. When you do, everyone is moving in the same direction. When you don't, you create opportunities to change yourself, your perspective, or your people. It's foolish for a leader to think they can ascribe underperformance to the individuals doing the work. Evaluation of underperformance must include an evaluation of the plan itself and how well leadership is driving it. The evaluation then goes all the way down through the organization to the individual level. If there's a bottleneck discovered at any point during this evaluation, it may create a necessity of moving people into other areas of the company or moving them out of the company altogether. Either way, leaders clear the blocks in the path to higher performance.

> The team in the Mountain region of Medtronic were seen within the company as a group of misfits or mavericks who were operating pretty much on their own. The data from the alignment survey clearly defined the problems within that region. The leadership goal became one of showing these employees a new strategy, getting them aligned *with purpose* to the mission and vision of the organization, and providing them with the means for delivering something significant and meaningful to the bottom line.
>
> To increase the bottom line, the team had to carve out market share from the competition. This was not an easy task. Before buy-in could be achieved from everyone, there were other issues to address.
>
> For example, there were certain pockets of people in parts of the region who were not receptive to my new leadership. Specifically, in some areas, there was not a high level of receptivity for a person of color coming in and running the show.
>
> In the case of the sales team members who were unreceptive to my leadership, the solution came in tying the team's goals and actions to the direction and broader mission of the organization. Once I aligned my efforts and actions to the mission and vision of the organization, it was made clear that anyone who went against the leadership (me) was, in essence, going

against the company. This was no longer a case of me, the new leader with no industry experience, setting goals for the team, but goals *for* and *by* the company that were tied to its mission and vision. This made it easier to either move dissatisfied individuals elsewhere within the company, where they *could* still make a contribution, or encourage them to work for the competition.

Ultimately, what was made clear to these employees was that when they didn't buy in to the strategic plan, they weren't just going against the leadership; they were choosing not to do what was right for the company, and, ultimately, for its patients. By operating from the point of what's in the best interests of the company and its clients, leaders can hold their heads high every time decisions are made.

Once Medtronic's reluctant employees understood that their alignment with the company depended on their alignment with their leader, everyone was on the same page and committed to the purpose. They each knew where their efforts impacted the results and were recognized and rewarded for their participation. There was buy-in. Even better, alignment was achieved, which generated a double-digit sales increase in market share.

This strategy has been highly visible in the political arena. Whether you agree with the tactic or not, historians point out that former President Barack Obama worked hard to be consistent with the ideals espoused in the Constitution. This made it difficult for frontal attacks by his adversaries. In essence, going against him was going against the Constitution.

It doesn't matter if the barrier to a leader's success is due to race, philosophy, or being perceived as an outsider. Any barrier will require time and attention before leadership can implement any new plans. What's clear is that it's critical to align the philosophies and direction of everyone in a manner congruent with the mission and vision of the broader organization.

When you're establishing a strategic plan, you're asking people to move forward and do something specific. If what you're asking them to do conflicts with what's expected at the broader organizational level or goes against the core values of the organization, you've put this person in a place of conflict. They're either going to have to interpret what they're going to do (lack of clarity), or they're going to create dissent within the organization. Both morale and momentum will be negatively impacted.

Any leader who invests the time to understand the process of setting strategic goals, establishing roles with purpose, and building out the strategies to implement a plan can achieve similar results. Leaders who can keep everyone moving forward on the same mission with purpose can—and will—be seen as great leaders.

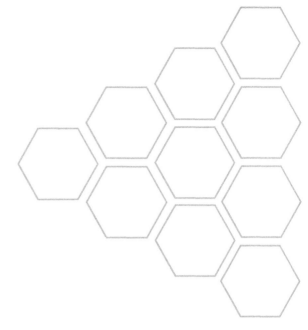

PART 2

THE NINE PILLARS
OF ALIGNMENT

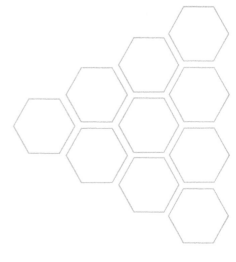

CHAPTER 4

INTRODUCTION TO THE NINE PILLARS OF ALIGNMENT

"The purpose of a team is not goal attainment but goal alignment."
– Tom DeMarco

L et's take a moment to liken the most important aspects of alignment to pillars. These pillars are critical to the strength of an organization and are designed to support all stakeholders as key components of organizational alignment. When one or more pillars are out of alignment, they can negatively impact the entire structure.

Nine pillars of alignment have been identified, and we'll touch on each of them in this section. Leaders must recognize and work to strengthen each, as necessary. All nine pillars require measurement to determine how they are impacting the organization's overall strategy and forward progress. An initial evaluation of the strength of each pillar will determine which areas are out of alignment and show leaders where to focus their efforts.

The Nine Pillars of Alignment

1. **Mission & Vision**: This is where leaders calibrate the compass and clarify a common goal or direction for the organization.
2. **Leadership**: Authenticity is critical. Leaders must demonstrate by example the expectations for everyone on the team. Authenticity is a case of monkey see/monkey do where indi-

viduals think, "If I see my boss behave a certain way, I feel I should do the same." This includes the manner with which communication is crafted and relayed.

3. **Communication**: This must be bi-directional and clear. The language used and the attenuation with which messages are delivered must be carefully monitored. Is there a need for a repeater down the line of the organization, or is the message strong and clear enough? Is there anything down the line of communication that could be hampering interpretation of the mission and vision?

4. **Accountability**: Each member of the team has 360-degree accountability. They are responsible to their peers, their leaders, and those further down the organizational chart, as well as to the end-user of the company's products.

5. **Empowerment**: Empowered individuals will be more confident and independent, not relying on leadership to micro-manage. Leaders encourage confidence and appreciate competence in individuals as they pertain to their roles. Rather than being a source of answers, leaders ask guiding questions that allow individuals to develop their own sound answers to questions that arise.

6. **Teamwork:** There are multiple teams within an organization. Successful alignment in this pillar relates to working within and across divisions and departments.

7. **Creativity:** This must be encouraged at every level of the organization as it is a precursor to innovation.

8. **Development:** There is an implicit agreement between employees and employers that the tools and training required to get the job done will be provided.

9. **Best Practices:** This involves constantly seeking out better ways of doing everything and implementing new strategic plans, processes, and systems that are in the best interest of the organization.

Organizational alignment is dependent upon the strength of each of these pillars. The level of alignment within each pillar is likely to vary, even in strongly aligned organizations. Leaders must constantly analyze each pillar and work to bring them into alignment before peak performance can be attained.

To get their arms around the initial level of organizational alignment, leaders must be willing to identify the one or two pillars that are most significantly impacting the organization in a negative manner and work on those first. Once identified, strategies and tactics can be developed to improve alignment within those pillars and generate relatively quick results.

Developing overarching alignment improvement strategies and specifying ways to integrate alignment into daily activities is critical to the success of every organization. Practice makes perfect. The more those within an organization ingrain alignment practices and philosophies into their culture, the better it is for all involved.

Accelerating Cultural Shift

Getting people to invest fully in achieving results is critical to accelerating cultural shift when an organization is out of alignment. Roger Connors and Tom Smith, authors of *Change the Culture, Change the Game*, call this "engaging it." Creating an environment for this shift to occur is the responsibility of leadership, as leaders are the agents of change.

It is important to note that are three levels of change within organizations. They are:

1. **Temporary change:** This type of change is implemented to attain a different result than the standard. Once accomplished, you will go back to how you did things before.
2. **Transitional change:** This type of change is to attain a sustained result for a specific period of time. Once the goal is accomplished, you may make an even greater forward change.
3. **Transformational change:** This involves change at the cultural level of an organization. Therefore, there's no question about where the organization is going. This type of change leads to alignment.

No matter which type of change is required, leaders need to be prepared to not only get individuals to engage in making the change, but to track those changes and reward them. In successful organizations, all positive behavior is rewarded, whether it's related to job roles, teamwork, innovations, development, or moving the needle toward improvement. All behaviors are evaluated for their benefit to the organization, and appropriate rewards are bestowed. As Hemingway said, "Never mistake motion for action." I would add to that to never mistake action for accomplishment, however. The actions rewarded must be positive.

Rewards may be as simple as individuals attaining self-satisfaction from doing the right thing. If the situation warrants it, rewards may be as involved as having leaders travel to deliver accolades, promotions, or perks in person, or in a very public manner such as a regional or national gathering. There is a reward for everything positive.

As a leader desirous of encouraging a cultural change that will lead to enhanced performance, the questions to ask are:

"What are employees getting for what they do?"

"What motivates them?"

To determine the best answers to these questions, leaders must understand where individuals are coming from. This is accomplished when leaders open lines of bi-directional communication (a.k.a. strengthening the *pillars* of leadership and communication).

Too often, leaders rely on the power of their positions—their authority, if you will—to extract accountability from others rather than empowering them to be accountable. Authentic accountability requires empowerment. To create such, leaders use their skills of asking questions about situations that arise versus defaulting to being reactive in providing answers. They encourage their peers, direct reports, and employees to experience feelings of empowerment by helping *them* be the ones to determine the best solutions for each situation. The experience of creating solutions will forge new beliefs in their abilities to do so, and beliefs drive behaviors. Behaviors and actions then lead to outcomes, and positive outcomes generate confidence in taking calculated risks in the future for the benefit of the organization without necessarily relying on leadership for all the answers.

How Alignment Issues Impact Turnover

Alignment improvement strategies are guided by the organization's metrics, which show both the overall direction and trajectory of alignment, as well as specific focal areas for improvement. These are connected to the high-level operational metrics that matter most to the organization—those that are tied to the mission and vision. That way, leadership decisions related to alignment improvement, including those which encourage alignment behaviors, will have the greatest impact.

How does this work in practice? Let's look at a common employer issue: voluntary employee turnover. Many studies show that people leave their jobs simply because they don't like their bosses. By looking deeper into this issue as it relates to alignment, it might be identified that the reason for voluntary departure often isn't just the boss. The reasons are because of multiple underlying issues the employee assumes are within the purview of the boss.

For example, it's entirely possible that an employee has left because he or she didn't feel empowered to do the job as expected. It might be that the employee was micromanaged. This would be linked to Pillar #2: Leadership. The employee may have seen that leaders didn't hold one another or the group accountable (Pillar #4). Many employees opt out because they don't feel valued. Some of these reasons could be the result of poor management, but in many instances, the culture of an organization stunts employee development or growth (Pillar #9). This can dramatically limit individual input or contribution.

> For many years, IBM fostered a culture of conformity. People were taught what to say and how and when to say it. They were expected to dress uniformly. For men, it was a navy suit, white shirt, conservative tie, and black wingtip shoes. It was a good fit for me early in my career.

As I matured and my career took off, I no longer needed to be bridled by the conformity required. I left IBM because the culture was no longer a fit for me, and Lexmark offered a progressive marketing and sales strategy.

Understanding individual motivations for voluntary departure is important in resolving this issue. Leaders cannot rely on the stock reason "because of the boss." Going deeper to discover areas of misalignment can help an organization develop culture changes that will inspire employees to stay. The degree to which everyone "buys into" alignment creates a common frequency among leaders and employees because everyone is working toward the same goals based on a common mission and vision connected to the organization. In this type of environment, people become more willing to communicate their expectations. Those expectations will be linked to the organization's alignment goals. The commitment to the organization will often override the option of defaulting to "leaving because of the boss."

With some issues, organizations can find it helpful to work with an outside source to objectively develop and provide a strategy and execution plan for achieving alignment based on the organization's overall mission and vision. The end goal, whether an external vendor is used or not, is to create buy-in around alignment from the entire leadership team—getting everyone "flying in formation" toward the same goal with maniacal focus. Then, the intentional and consistent process of cascading and imbuing alignment goals and practices throughout the organization becomes easier, more impactful, and longer-lasting.

Let's consider how enterprise-wide alignment relates to the pillar of accountability, which directly impacts turnover. In general, the more activities and energy that are put into accountability in an organization, the greater the reduction in voluntary turnover. Leaders, managers, and individuals who are accountable have more mental and emotional "skin in the game." Those who are not accountable just won't care enough to stay.

Lateral Alignment

Another advantage of working toward alignment in each of the pillars within the organization is that leaders broaden their focus. They begin looking beyond themselves and their own roles to their peers and thinking laterally, which benefits all. With lateral thinking, answers are sought to the question: "How do we go about acting as if we are each other's internal customers and doing what it takes to satisfy those customers in the context of our organization's mission, vision, and strategic plan?" When that happens, the common frequency of the mission, vision, and strategic plan becomes the mantra around *all* of the pillars that drive the behaviors you are after. All alignment pillars are impacted when this lateral thinking occurs because the language used is common. There's more interaction and collaboration across teams, and employees at all levels understand how they, individually, impact both the mission and their customers.

An ancillary benefit to lateral alignment is that it dramatically reduces leadership stress levels. When there is lateral alignment, the focus then is to drive alignment longitudinally throughout the organization. This is where further development of the communication pillar comes into play with a focus on messaging and attenuation.

The biggest challenge in getting management teams aligned is competing objectives. This behavior may be due to difficulties arising from the introduction of new strategies or a workplace culture that engenders reactionary mentalities and behaviors such as public humiliation for making a mistake.

Keeping the Mission and Vision Front and Center

Actions to improve individual accountability range from keeping the mission and vision statements front and center to hiring an executive or personal coach. The coach's responsibility is to help the leader or employee connect their life's purpose to the mission and vision. The more these correlate, the greater the alignment. In holding other employees accountable, we have to be careful not to offend. Not everyone appreciates "internal affairs." The culture police can drive accountability by asking effective, thought-provoking questions. Just imagine what might happen when managers and leaders at every level engage with individuals this way. These thought-provoking questions require intentionality and introspection but can lead to meaningful dialogue, improving communication and accountability.

As the previous example about creating a culture of accountability demonstrated, leaders play an integral role in achieving such goals. Leaders must explain, in several different ways and over a prolonged period, how making these changes will prove beneficial to everyone and lead to a more positive work culture for all. With this type of approach, improving accountability now becomes a standard, not a directive, with everyone encouraged to lean in.

Conversely, if you are leading in a command-and-control style and stating directives to employees without trying to get buy-in, not only will your efforts likely not succeed, your turnover rate will likely increase. We see this with many of our law enforcement clients. By failing to connect their everyday work with their mission and vision, they undercut their ability to achieve their goals. We often see employees doing the bare minimum of work in these types of cultures.

Accountability

Now, let's talk about the process of achieving organizational alignment around accountability. Organizations that have a strong sense of accountability have a correlating complement of empowerment. Before an organization can have accountability, its leaders need to have empowerment. When leaders buy into new strategies of alignment *because they believe it is the right thing to do*, they will not only do a better job but will continue being accountable and drive the behavior down into the lowest levels of the organization. Most people will go the extra mile to do good work when it's something they *want to do* versus something they have been *told to do*. Accountability is an acknowledgment of stakeholder needs, and the degree of stakeholder satisfaction becomes the scorecard. Effective leaders are able to establish a pride of ownership mentality among employees through empowerment.

> My dad was the CEO of a metal finishing company. I remember him having a conversation with the janitor and helping him load supplies on his cart. The janitor was quite surprised with the assistance provided. After chatting for a few moments, my dad said to him, "I don't mind helping you do this, but, in turn, I want your help. I want to know how I might do my job better." I watched that janitor's energy level increase as soon as that request was made. Here was the CEO asking for his help, his opinion. It created a new sense of pride for the company in the janitor!

When leaders visit a shop floor to speak with individuals rather than sending for them, it says to the individuals, "I understand how important your job is. I don't want to interrupt your work." When that same leader notices and picks up some trash, they demonstrate attention to detail and a desire to care about the work environment. This type of behavior demonstrates to everyone around them that no one is above taking action in moving the organization in the direction it needs to go.

When employees know what needs to be done and know how to do it, the typical things that get in the way are resentment, which speaks to being undervalued or unnoticed, and personal integrity. In other words, "This work conflicts with my norms or values." Strong leaders are able to identify and rectify these alignment challenges quickly.

When an organization's leadership does not invest time and effort into developing a high level of accountability, it's important that leaders help employees understand that effort and outcome are very different.

Let's reflect on your business. What are the opportunities within your organization to shift the mindset of your teams so that they are aligned with the vast opportunities within your industry? Answer these four questions about your business and reflect on how you can improve accountability throughout your organization.

1. Does every employee know all of the stakeholders to which they are accountable?
2. To what degree do you seek constructive feedback from each stakeholder?
3. To what extent do you provide constructive feedback to your peers?
4. What mechanism/method do you employ to ensure feedback received gets implemented?

There are specific questions related to each pillar of alignment, which we will continue to go over as we move through this book. However, it is ultimately up to the leadership of the organization to ensure the questions are being asked and answered in their quest to achieve the benefits of increased alignment.

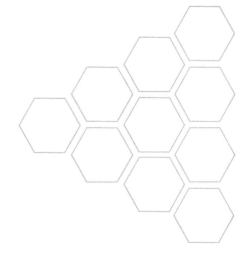

CHAPTER 5

MISSION AND VISION

"Fundamentally, your mission becomes your constitution,
the solid expression of your vision and values. It becomes
the criterion by which you measure everything else."
– Stephen Covey

The path to success for any organization begins with establishing a mission and vision. The purpose of the mission is to define the organization, what it is about, and what it will do. The vision, on the other hand, is what the world will look like when the organization succeeds. The mission's purpose should be understood and embraced by everyone within the organization. Its success is dependent upon employees' understanding of how their efforts relate to the mission and add value to the lives of their customers.

When employees are aligned with their organization's mission and vision, they see and experience purpose in their daily work. They know how their individual, daily efforts contribute to desired outcomes. When leaders weave the organization's mission and vision into the fabric of every communication, it deepens the employees' purpose and accelerates performance. When there is little or no employee alignment around an organization's mission and vision, employees don't truly understand what's going on in the organization outside their daily "to-do" lists. There is no personal connection to the success of the company or to the customers.

Alignment to the Mission

Employee alignment to the mission is demonstrated in both big and small ways. As an example, police forces generally have a mission to enhance public trust while serving their communities. That is the broad mission. It needs to be fulfilled within certain parameters due to the nature of public safety agencies. However, the little ways police officers live out that mission, based on how they go about their business, are what matters most to a community.

In the minds of the people they serve, the response should be favorable to the following questions:

1. Are members of the police force consistent in their actions in the community?
2. Are they respectful in their interactions?
3. Do they regularly demonstrate that they are worthy of public support?

The answers to questions like these determine whether the police force is matching their mission. When the answers to those three questions are positive, public trust is likely strong, and the mission is being fulfilled.

Clear and Simple Mission

Your organization's mission must be clear and straightforward. Every employee should understand and be able to rattle it off at a moment's notice. It's also important to make the mission memorable, so it is consistently represented through every employee's efforts. When situations arise that require adjustments to the current processes or structure of an organization, or how to interact with customers, the mission will be taken into consideration.

Here are just a few examples of simple, yet clear mission statements:

- **Medtronic**: "We alleviate pain, restore health and extend life."
- **Colorado Springs School District**: "We dare to empower the whole student to profoundly impact our world."
- **Anoka County (Minnesota) Sheriff's Office**: "To protect and serve the community in a manner that preserves the public trust."
- **General Mills**: "To make lives healthier, easier and richer."
- **Las Vegas Metropolitan Police Department**: "To protect the community through prevention, partnership, and professional service."

How clear is your mission? If you're uncertain of the answer to this question, it's time to survey your fellow leaders, managers, individuals, and customers to determine what they think it means and make any necessary adjustments to ensure you're delivering the intended message.

How to Keep the Mission Front and Center

How well do you currently weave your organization's mission into your communications? If you're unsure, here are some suggestions:

1. Mention the mission in all internal communications. Tie every process, plan, and action back to it, both verbally and visually.
2. Speak with leaders in every department to learn of stories that exemplify efforts supporting the mission. Learn about circumstances, players, conflicts, actions, and results. Gain a solid understanding of situations in which departments or individuals hit or missed the mark by acting in accordance with the mission and vision. Then, determine any accolades that should be offered or changes that should be made, and let the rest of the organization know.
3. Recognize individuals, teams, and other leaders for actions that connect with the mission and vision. It's especially important to recognize leaders who are often overlooked for their efforts as being "expected."
4. Formally recognize those who demonstrate the ideals of the mission and vision. This type of recognition could be as simple as a highlight in an internal communication or an inexpensive reward.

5. Post the mission everywhere. It should appear on the walls of the organization, on coffee mugs, luggage tags, notepads, pens—practically every surface with which the team interacts! Lastly, it should be a part of every individual's email signature.

When Changes Are Required

When leaders create new strategic plans for their organizations, it's important that they tie these plans to the mission and develop a communication strategy to support them. In other words, leaders must agree laterally on parameters for how the leadership team will present the new plan throughout the organization. The plan must not be delivered as an edict from above, but instead based on how it supports the organization's mission. Furthermore, it must be consistent. Any missteps in consistency can derail an organization or, in extreme cases, even lead to jail time.

Leaders cannot assume strategic plans will be accepted by one and all unless (and until) everyone understands how they relate to the mission of the organization. To get feedback on whether or not a plan is understood, it's a good idea to reach out to benchmark people—those who are looked up to within teams or divisions, whether they have the title of "leader" or not. These may be strong team players who are committed to getting the job done with excellence. They are likely to have high credibility within the organization. Determine how they are interpreting the plan and how it relates to the overall mission of the organization. By getting feedback, it may come to light that additional clarification is needed.

Even when your messaging is clear and there appears to be strong buy-in for strategic plans within teams, the link to the mission will need to be reinforced at regular intervals. In reporting on the progress of strategic plans, address how individual contributions are meeting the mission and how the vision of what the world will look like is coming into focus.

When communication of mission and vision are clear and consistent, perceptions of leadership improve. This brings forth alignment in this pillar, and everyone rallies around the same vision of what the future will look like when the organization succeeds.

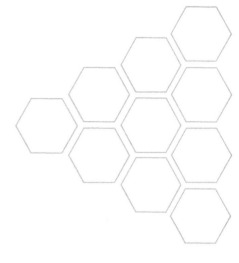

CHAPTER 6

LEADERSHIP

"Leadership is having a compelling vision,
a comprehensive plan, relentless implementation,
and talented people working together."
– Alan Mulally

L eadership is something that is measured to help ascertain the degree to which a leader is not only effective in terms of outcome, but also of perception. How do others in the organization perceive that organization through its leadership? Do those in leadership positions have the technical prowess to truly understand how their words and actions impact the organization as a whole? Do they have the ability to look at the big picture and break it down into bite-sized pieces so others in the organization can digest it? The consistency of communication from leadership can easily be measured, and it's always in line with how good leaders are at selling the vision—both inside and outside the organization—to create a groundswell of support.

The construct of leadership is multifaceted. By the nature of the roles, those in leadership positions are more often in the limelight. Because of their exposure, leaders are watched and evaluated at every turn by their peers, their direct reports, and employees down the line. All of these people have livelihoods and personal lives that are impacted by leadership decisions and actions. Therefore, the most important concept for leaders to understand is how those decisions and actions affect others, and to keep that understanding at the forefront of their communications. The most effective leaders understand that every interaction with a person or group has the chance to either strengthen or break down bonds of trust, connection, and alignment.

One of the first hurdles leaders must overcome in gaining the support of others is to prove authenticity. The questions in the minds of others are:

"Are they who they say they are?"

"Do they demonstrate that?"

Inauthentic leaders are hard to follow and impossible to trust—the tactical aspects of doing business fall flat when authenticity is not present.

Many leaders of the past have tried to associate integrity with trust, i.e., "I have integrity; therefore, you should trust me." That concept may be acceptable to some of their peers and direct reports, but whether or not to trust a leader really comes down to predictability. Integrity varies for most people, depending upon the issue at hand. On the other hand, trust and predictability are akin to one another. It's possible to trust someone whose values don't match yours. What *truly* matters is whether or not they're predictable—if they are who they say they are and will do what they say they will.

The person to trust least is someone who is unpredictable. When people are predictable, even if we don't like their values, attitudes, or skillsets, we can work with or around those knowns. We can move them to where their perceived weaknesses or challenges will do little to no harm to the organization.

Leading by Example

The way in which leaders handle *their* roles will be reflected in how everyone else handles their own roles. Notice is taken when leaders are notoriously late to meetings. Such actions, whether done consciously or unconsciously, are disrespectful of the other attendees. Those actions send a message that the leader's time is more important than everyone else's. They may also send a message that the leader would rather be elsewhere or involved in something else—that the purpose of the meeting is not important. This contributes to lowered morale and a reduction of trust from those most impacted by what the meetings are to cover. Being late to meetings also demonstrates an inability to manage time. This makes it hard for the leader to demand quality time management from others.

Sadly, many in leadership positions like the notion of being followed. What too many fail to comprehend is that when you have a group of followers, they may "follow" all of your actions—even the bad ones. This is not to say that leaders have to be perfect. It just means that they must be aware of how everything they communicate gets interpreted.

Rather than having a mindset of "I'm the leader. Others have to follow me and go along with my decisions," it's critical that leaders understand that their roles within the organization are much the same as the role of the organization in the marketplace. They are there to serve the needs of their customers. For leaders, the customers are the internal team members. When leaders "expect" or "demand" adherence to their decisions, employees don't feel their input is valued. They do not feel empowered, and they will hesitate to make what might be tremendously valuable contributions to the organizations. Thus, it's far better for leaders to be able to admit their faults and weaknesses—seeking others with the strength to balance the load—than letting their egos get in the way of organizational performance.

Tapping into the Experiences of Others

In the book *Change the Culture, Change the Game* by Roger Connors and Tim Smith, they cover the concept of how beliefs and expectations bring forth actions and results. A transformational leader knows that their actions need to be focused on understanding—and framing—the experiences and beliefs of employees as they pertain to the actions taken and behaviors shown toward meeting the mission and vision.

Transformational leaders don't assume they know best. They assume they can *discover* what's best through bi-directional communication. They seek opportunities to empower others to do great things and enjoy the process of doing so. They are able to look at what ails an organization without judgment or blame. They remain focused on removing stumbling blocks and creating environments in which performance can accelerate. They are open and willing to invest the time to get to know their peers, directs, and individuals on the team. Transformational leaders remain true to the mission of the organization while doing whatever is within their power to create alignment.

To get employees (and fellow leaders) aligned, leaders must tap into the experiences and beliefs of others. With that understanding, leaders then know what might need adjusting in order to connect that person more tightly to the *why* of the organization. When asked, most team members are more than happy to let leadership know what they most want, need, and expect from them in order to perform at their highest levels. When employees are helped to see how their beliefs and experiences match the mission and vision, they will be able to formulate how they can act in an aligned manner, which will bring the needed results.

Leadership Styles

What style of leadership best suits you, your organization, your peers, direct reports, or anyone else on your team? The answer might vary depending upon your type of organization or the situations in which you find yourself. What's important is to understand the benefit of the different leadership styles, recognize which style is appropriate for each circumstance, and then use it.

1. **The Servant Leadership Style**

   Servant leaders are keenly focused on the overall success and development of individuals and teams versus their own success. They understand that the success of those they serve will benefit them personally in the end. Along with removing roadblocks and barriers to performance, servant leaders look to help employees discover their full potentials and then to fuel intrinsic motivations within people to accelerate that potential. Servant leaders find out what people want and need, then work to deliver it.

2. **The One-Minute Manager® Style**

   This style, outlined in Ken Blanchard's book by the same name,[2] is powerful in encouraging empowerment and driving decision-making down through the organization. Driving down this authority to the lowest possible level will connect employees more to what the company does and make them feel more like they are making solid contributions. There should be less bureaucracy and micromanagement with this style of leadership. However, if proper controls and solid management are not in place, inconsistencies can create havoc.

3. **The Shepherd Leadership Style**

   In this style, the leaders identify which other leaders or team members have the skills and commitment to take the organization farther and faster. Then, these leaders shepherd everyone else on the team to get behind those people—giving those performance leaders the support and resources they need to get the job done. This type of leader does not take the bull by the horns or issue directives. Instead, they empower those within the organization who have more knowledge and skill to get the mission accomplished and lead from behind.

4. **The Command-and-Control Leadership Style**

This is the type of leadership more familiar to past generations. Leaders tell the employees what to do and how to do it through directives issued from above. The employees are viewed as resources used to drive output. While it was (and still is) an effective form of leadership in some sectors, many of today's workers find it oppressive.

Instances where this style of leadership is warranted include law enforcement and the military. This style can be necessary when all aspects of situations need to be managed "by the book." It's best used in cases where very specific procedures must be followed, such as OSHA regulations, to prevent serious injury or mishaps.

To illustrate the difference in the results generated by two very different leadership styles, here is the story of two sister companies.

A Canadian parent company had two affiliate companies. One company was based in the U.S., the other in the U.K. One was much larger than the other, but their operational workflows were similar. The big difference between the two were the leadership styles. Both companies were migrating their enterprise resource planning (ERP) systems to something new.

The U.S-based company took great pains to prepare each impacted function for what this ERP migration meant to them, what the benefit would be, and how they may have to adjust the way they conducted their business. One of the most-impacted areas was the order-to-cash function. The order processing and customer service areas knew they would have a tough time being successful at their jobs with the new system if they didn't take care of the garbage entered into the system over the years. (It's that old "garbage-in, garbage-out" story.)

The leadership listened to the end-users and worked with every level to map out what was needed. Input was received on how processes could be modified to make everything work more smoothly in the new system. These conversations were coordinated with the technology teams to make certain what was expected of the new ERP and what was needed to accomplish those expectations within the technology.

A communication committee was created that included all impacted areas. There were constant, in-depth discussions about how things would be changing. The goal was to determine how internal and external communications could be initiated to make the launch successful. The result of having aligned leadership behind the plan was that disruptions were kept to a minimum. Customers were not significantly impacted, and business continued to flow. The implementation wasn't perfect, and the ERP continued to require regular updates to meet the needs of business. But, overall, the change was well-handled by all.

The sister company in the U.K. didn't fare as well. It did not choose to use the same version of the ERP system that the U.S. did, rejecting all the experience and modifications that had occurred. Leaders decided not to modify their processes to fit the system, nor did they work in advance to clean up data.

The leadership of the company was involved in committee meetings, but there was little interest in committing to the process as the decision to make the change wasn't theirs. It had been placed upon them by the parent company. In fact, as the ERP was ready to launch, there was a "go/no-go" meeting called for by the top leadership. The potential ramifications of the launch were discussed. Only half of the leadership team attended. And, even though those who did attend understood the business-critical issues that would likely result, they chose to move forward. Product didn't ship out for six weeks because the system did not have enough lines available to populate the entire address on labels. The system was unable to print packing slips, and there were shipping problems for several months as the company tried to make corrections and clean out garbage in the system.

As you might imagine, many blamed the ERP system when the fault truly fell on the shoulders of the leadership. For the U.S. company, the desire to improve the system was internal, not forced upon them. The parent company dictated the decision for the U.K. from the top down. The U.S. company invested the time and effort to understand the impact of the change and to get in front of it. The U.K. team didn't buy into the change and made decisions in accordance with that attitude. The difference in leadership styles and engagement generated widely different levels of performance and results.

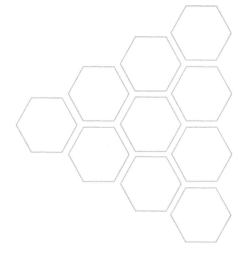

CHAPTER 7

COMMUNICATION

"Communication is the real work of leadership."
– Nitin Nohria

Each person has an ideal set of frequencies in which they are most comfortable communicating. Accountants have certain frequencies, whereas salespeople lean on different ones. This is likened to radio frequencies or the selections of "moods" or genres within music streaming apps. When a frequency is not appropriate for the audience, it can cause a disconnect to take place. To create alignment in communication, strong leaders develop skills to communicate across a large number of frequencies or within multiple genres. Developing strong communication skills requires practice and consistent effort.

Communication, or more specifically, miscommunication, is responsible for more errors in decision-making and implementation in organizations than any other reason. Effective communication is central to the success of every relationship and organization. It is at the core of every other aspect of alignment.

In organizations where communication is aligned, the overall mission is discussed with regularity and incorporated into everything operationally. It leads to everyone being on the same page, or tuned to the same channel, no matter their job position or personal communication styles. Employees freely share and collect success stories with one another to connect everyone to the organization's vision and mission. Such stories create more meaningful workplace experiences and help change employee beliefs in ways that make them more dedicated and connected to their jobs. This is a recurring dynamic, with success stories begetting additional success stories down the road.

Communication as a Building Block of Organizational Alignment

Effective communication is critical to driving alignment and success at all levels. Communications expert Bill Quirke, author of *Making the Connections*, tells us, "when employees understand their overall role in business, 91 percent will work towards its success. But when they don't, that figure drops sharply to just 23 percent."[3] A 2010 study concluded that over a five-year period, the returns to shareholders by companies with "highly effective internal communication" exceeded returns by the "least effective companies" by 47 percent.[4] It's simple.

Highly effective communication is a requirement of success. Poor communication hinders it.

The absence of effective communication within an organization can manifest in many ways:

- Lack of accountability in employees and finger-pointing
- Indifference to customers
- Missed opportunities for innovation
- Poor levels of collaboration
- Emergence of unofficial communication channels (grapevines) that distort information and present biased views
- Negative morale
- Resentment among employees
- Disengagement

Any of these issues can derail the forward progress of an organization in implementing strategic plans.

How Communication Impacts Alignment

George Bernard Shaw said, "The single biggest problem in communication is the illusion that it has taken place." Miscommunication can be a pitfall between two individuals and can multiply exponentially in the context of organizational communication.

Many individuals practice one-way communication. Their thinking is, "If I've said it, it's been communicated." Communication is only achieved when the recipient of it comprehends the message and signals their level of comprehension back to the sender. This is what's called a feedback loop. When feedback loops are utilized, communicators can verify that messages have been acknowledged and comprehended, or if further information or clarification is required. Further evidence of effective communication is when proper actions are taken. Feedback loops encourage open dialogue between levels and peers alike.

When leaders do not communicate effectively, teams and individuals are forced to translate messages to their frequencies of understanding. This could result in counter-productive actions as meanings get "lost in translation."

Getting Communication Right

Leaders who have developed the soft skills of effective communication are—and will continue to be—in high demand. There are many elements involved, and constantly improving these skills requires proficiency in the following:

- Encouraging a culture of open, multi-directional communication, no matter what the message is
- Using clear, direct, jargon-free messaging
- Delivering message channels appropriate to the audience and the message
- Disseminating accurate and consistent information
- Speaking at the right frequency for your audience
- Bridging the gap across cultures, languages, and time zones
- Demonstrating integrity by doing or causing to happen that which has been promised

Leaders will do well to analyze their effectiveness in each of those elements of communication. Honesty and openness are required if leaders are to improve these skills and grow in their abilities to lead.

One of the roles of leaders is to assist in the development of other leaders. To promote effective communication through others, teach them best practices in the pillar of communication. These include:

- What to communicate: the messages and their priority
- How to communicate: what channels are appropriate to each audience, situation, and message
- When to communicate: immediate communication can deter the development of negative or incorrect information
- Where to communicate: some messages should be delivered publicly; others privately

Communication Gaps

In high-performing organizations, both teams and individuals regularly receive feedback and recognition for their performance as it relates to goals within the organization. However, well-aligned organizations use communication to collaborate, reach consensus, engage in respectful conflict, remove silos, and create opportunities for one another and the success of the company. Channels of communication are well-established and used effectively. That's the ideal world for achieving alignment in the area of communication. However, few companies or departments operate consistently at this level. The question then becomes, "Why?"

Most organizations operate with a moderate or low level of discussion internally about their mission and vision.

I once conducted an experiment with a group of about 40 MBA candidates at Villanova. Most were working full-time in the corporate world. Each candidate was offered $100 to recite, verbatim, the mission statement of their company. Not one of them was able to do it. Granted, this was a small group. However, their lack of ability to recite their company's mission likely translates to a lack of commitment to the mission of the company that is paying for their MBA program. Let that sink in!

In their 2001 book, *The Strategy-Focused Organization*, Robert Kaplan and David Norton reported that "a mere seven percent of employees today fully understand their company's business strategies and what's expected of them in order to help achieve company goals." What seems to be missing is the attention by leaders to the notion of "organizational alignment"—which is about ensuring that your people are always in tune with the organization's vision and strategies—and are thus working to achieve the desired results. This lack of organizational alignment points to a lack of clear communication.

In misaligned organizations, communication about goal progress happens sporadically, usually just at quarterly or annual meetings. It was noted through a test group that more than half of all employees were unclear about the progress made toward the organization's goals. This phenomenon persists when communication channels are not bi-directional and are conflicted with personal bias. What gets lost is leadership's opportunity to connect the organization's purpose with the work to be done. That connection is made and reinforced through success stories.

In misaligned organizations, few success stories are shared. Communication practices and channels are inconsistent or irregularly used, and there's little consistency between leaders connecting the organization's purpose with the work to be done. However, this isn't done out of malice. It's typically due to being in a perpetual state of busyness, wedded with ignorance over the true power and impact of proper communication.

When this level of haphazard and substandard communication occurs within an organization, employees are typically left wondering and often "wandering" without understanding the connection between their daily work and the greater vision and mission of the organization. They just "do their work." In the absence of official communications, internal factions or groups tend to create their own stories, which often aren't positive and may hinder the good work being done.

The worst scenario for communication discord reflects a total disconnect among employees. No one has enough information to know whether they're contributing to the organization's success, or even if the organization is successful at all. This plays out time after time at annual employee meetings. To kick off the new year or launch a new product, presenters discuss the success of the company, but the employees are thinking:

1. Why am I here?
2. How does this correlate to what I do on a day to day basis?
3. Should I be doing something different when I go back to work?

When leaders don't answer these questions, they have done employees a disservice. There is little to no feedback from managers, and the development of processes is left to individuals. Often, communication channels simply don't exist—other than the ever-present, unreliable, and at times grievance-bearing grapevine.

Where communication is lacking, mistrust thrives, especially in workplaces that have regular downtime opportunities for employees to sit or stand around and gab. Employees spend more time wondering about what's going on than getting things done.

Ideally, beneficial communication in an organization should be both bi-directional and multi-directional. This means that communications should occur regularly between two individuals (bi-directional) as well as multiple individuals (multi-directional). Information moves freely and naturally in a healthy organization, both up and down the communication chain. When messages of what to do and how to do it only flow in one direction from the top down, the organization becomes more like a fiefdom or dictatorship. While some employees thrive on being told what to do, most do not. In organizations that thwart free-flowing communication, top talent will emigrate to other organizations where their input and feedback are appreciated.

Encoding and Decoding Communication

Leaders will do well to understand the power and value of encoding and decoding the quality of their communications. Both aspects of communication involve converting a message into the most palatable form for its recipients. When we talk about "encoding," what we're looking for are the answers to these three questions:

1. What is the message quality? Is it appropriate for the audience?
2. Is the message clear, and is its frequency proper along the lines of tone, volume, tenor, and pace? How might this message be misinterpreted?
3. Has it been verified that the message was received?

With experience, leaders will automatically weigh all communications against these three questions. They will establish expectations of feedback beyond "Yes, we got the message." They will anticipate real feedback on the level of comprehension of the message either in the form of direct communication or by the actions of the recipients.

From the decoding perspective of communication, leadership moves to a deeper level by continuing to relay the message throughout the organization. They will constantly evaluate these three questions:

1. Have we acknowledged receipt of the message?
2. Have we clarified any ambiguities or inconsistencies, not leaving anything to misinterpretation? Does it conflict with anything else that's been said?
3. Is there a feedback loop for relevant feedback to be provided and considered?

Once the answers to all three of these questions are positive, communication can be deemed as clear and the most effective actions toward the goal should follow.

Three Levels of Aligned Communication

Communication alignment is not something that one person can accomplish. In fact, it is something that must happen throughout the organization. While it requires a communal effort, there are usually different levels of communication required in most organizations.

1. **From the top down**. This is the communication that lays the groundwork for consistency within the entire group. Provide a clear message, including language to be used as the message is cascaded down through the organization. This is not unlike the "spin" that is put on marketing messages.

2. **Between teams**. Communication between teams can be latitudinal—between departments. It can also be longitudinal. The longitudinal aspect is often seen in school districts, as an example, where there is a disconnect between the district office and the actual site, which would be the school. The pushback from the site can be something along the lines of, "The people at the district office may have been in my role before, but they no longer know what we're faced with on a day-to-day basis." The district office mentality may be one of, "I have arrived. All of these wonderful ideas I have can now be implemented." In some cases, those at the district level are unable to convey their ideas to the leaders of the schools in such a manner that the principals see the benefit of implementing them.

3. **Individual communication.** This may be between a leader and employee or between employees. These messages need to be consistent with top-level communication, as well. If they are not consistent, people will see the discrepancies and wonder what should be done. Consider this theory by sales

trainer Tom Hopkins that, "A confused mind says 'no.'" In other words, when people aren't clear about the next step, they take none.

An example of a discrepancy that can take place at the highest level of an organization is where a vice president has been told they have a strategic role in an organization's success, but their department or project gets under-funded. This can cause an internal resource grab or create internal resource hoarders. The employees within this organization see completely different behavior than what's being expressed.

When leaders across functions communicate in similar ways, connecting all messages with the mission and vision, the entire organization will have a common thread. Even if there is turnover, this culture of communication will help the organization stay its course.

Communication with Millennials

A perfect example of employee dissatisfaction over communications comes with the entry of millennials to the workforce. While millennials' elders may have been satisfied to simply hold jobs and be able to "bring home the bacon," millennials are not. They heard their parents, grandparents, and other elders complain about being mere cogs in someone else's machinery and were admonished not to accept similar fates.

A large part of millennials' rationale for working is centered around purpose. They want their jobs or careers to have meaning in the greater scheme of things. They want their voices and opinions to be heard, and to matter. If they are not able to share their thoughts and ideas within the organization, they will take their skills elsewhere.

If there is a high level of turnover in organizations, not just with millennials, but in every part of your workforce, ask yourself these questions:

- "Are we really listening to the employee base, in terms of ways that we can do things differently?"
- "What input can be generated from individuals that can positively impact the forward movement of the organization?"
- "Are our leaders communicating in a way that connects all employees to how they impact the mission and vision?"

The answers to these questions speak to the importance of equity and financial reward to the organization that gets all employees aligned. In other words, how might corporate financials look if no one in the organization felt marginalized? This is where bi-directional communication moves your organization into alignment.

When leadership and employees communicate well with one another, everyone wins. In many organizations, one department or division is responsible for a single aspect of product development. Their roles could involve creating products or simply accumulating that product's raw materials. Whatever the role, once that division has completed its responsibilities, the balance of the work is then moved to another department or division. In these situations, communication becomes critical to make handoffs and linkages as smooth as possible. Each department, then, is an internal customer to the other. The degree to which we delight our internal customers is a barometer of success. The old saying related to "getting our house in order first" is applicable here.

If a change in raw materials is necessary, and the division that is required to work with these materials does not receive advance communications about the change, the end result could be disastrous. The organization's equipment may not be able to handle the new raw materials, or the end product could end up being of a lesser quality. All sorts of challenges could arise. However, when communication flows well between divisions, whether at the leadership level or among individuals within the departments, such challenges can be avoided, and the company as a whole benefits.

Communication Challenges Specific to the Public Sector

The public sector has different but equal challenges in communication. What often occurs in public sector jobs is that those in administration lose sight of the "customer" and how best to serve them. Leaders get caught up internally and isolate themselves from the general public they are supposed to serve. For example, in education, the superintendent's role is to give principals and teachers the tools they need to get their job done, which is about connecting with students in ways that allow them to learn and succeed. When a school district's mission and vision around student success are kept at the forefront of all communications, there is greater success at all levels. But when the superintendent, principals, and teachers forget or neglect their customers and focus more on their own internal needs, everyone falters or fails.

When organizations set forth their mission and vision as a common element for employees to rally behind, their perceptions of leadership and the organization improve. Employees feel empowered to make wise decisions. There's less micromanagement. People feel more personally accountable and are willing to hold others accountable—for the benefit of all stakeholders. This all begins with establishing effective communication channels that are open and accepting of feedback from all directions. These channels must be continuously monitored for occlusion due to personal bias and competing or conflicting messaging or attenuation due to the strength and quality of the message along with the frequency with which those messages are sent.

The greatest benefit of strengthening this pillar of communication is that everyone understands the language being used and tunes in at the same frequency. The end result is the clear reception of messages being delivered throughout the organization, which eliminates confusion, increases performance, and can lower turnover.

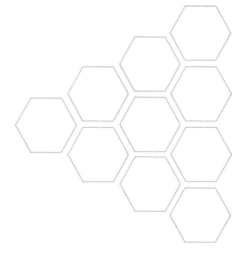

CHAPTER 8

ACCOUNTABILITY

*"Accountability separates the wishers in life from
the action-takers that care enough about their
future to account for their daily actions."*
– John Di Lemme

Accountability is the ability and willingness to take owner-ship of outcomes arising from one's attitudes, behaviors, and consequent choice of actions. Implicit in the definition is the expectation that individuals who exhibit accountability do not make excuses or blame others for things that are *their* responsibility. Even with things that are not within their realm of responsibility, individuals actively contribute to the good of the organization in an accountable manner.

Accountability is a construct that is central to alignment because what it speaks to is that everyone understands their roles and responsibilities in the organization. They are mindful of how they are performing against the objectives that have been established as the metrics of success, as well as where they are on the continuum of achieving goals and objectives. When everyone commits to being accountable for their roles in an organization, this is a 360-degree concept. Each person is accountable to every other person their actions impact—all stakeholders.

This level of accountability gives leaders an opportunity to see how everyone is performing and have clear conversations around any shortcomings. As an example, when workers are accountable and a faulty component is discovered on the factory floor, it is brought to the attention of those who can do something about it. There is no finger-pointing or blame thrown at the designers, suppliers, equipment, or operators, nor are they ignoring it with the thinking, "That's not my job." The thought process is one of, "It *is* my job to help the organization fulfill its mission, even if what I discover does not fall within my role."

When a store assistant in one section of a department store is not busy and voluntarily helps customers in another section find what they are looking for, the store benefits from their attitude of shared accountability. At one popular department store chain, this has been termed "The Nordstrom Way." This strategy is an excellent demonstration of accountability in action. Nordstrom encourages everyone on its staff to use their own initiative to deliver exceptional customer service.

More importantly, the company stands behind employees for taking the lead in *delighting* customers.

As a trait, accountability spans both personal and professional lives. It goes beyond knowing one's responsibilities. It is what makes individuals do what it takes to achieve the desired outcomes while complying with all applicable laws, company policies, and societal norms. It requires both willingness and ability to take ownership of one's actions and their consequences.

Leadership's Role in Accountability

Within the alignment pillar of accountability, leaders must address both sides of the topic. They must be willing to measure how accountable *they* are to the mission and vision, first and foremost. Only then should they begin to analyze and improve the level of accountability of others. There are two primary questions to ask within this realm of accountability, and they are both immediately actionable.

1. "To what extent do I, as a leader, hold myself accountable to the goals within my role, the organization's mission, and its vision?"
2. "To what extent do employees hold one another accountable to meet goals and act in accordance with the mission and vision?"

When employees become aligned around the mission and vision, and their individual purpose is congruent to it, everyone contributes at a higher level of performance, and the pace of change, improvement, and productivity accelerates. As we understand the responses to those two questions about account-ability and start implementing measures to increase it—as well as empowerment and the other pillars—signs of improvement will become obvious, which will then lead to documentable evidence.

Documenting evidence of accountability can be as simple as using a spreadsheet to track commitments versus actions. This is all part of project managing our way to success—when we are getting granular about the actions that need to be carried out to fulfill the mission. It's a simple method of tracking whether or not the necessary actions are being taken by all.

When there's a disconnect between what's been agreed upon and what actions are taken, this type of scorecard makes it very clear. The role of leadership then becomes one of com-municating with the others involved to determine why action is not going according to plan. It could be that some of those involved haven't really bought into the plan, or there might be obstacles preventing them from taking action. Effective com-munication will uncover the challenges and improve the level of accountability.

Leaders who aim to build and sustain high-performance organizations must know that although accountability is largely a personal trait, the consistency with which it finds expression in the workplace is the result of how well the leaders themselves walk the talk. When organizations set minimal expectations for leadership, the message to the broader organization is that underperformance is acceptable. A CEO who looks for scape-goats when the mission is not clear or the strategic plan is faulty can hardly expect members of his or her organization to be exemplars of accountability.

Leaders must set the standard and live by it themselves. It's one thing to have personal accountability as a leader. It's another to create an environment where individual accountability leads to shared accountability throughout the organization. The end result of shared accountability is an attitude of "We sink or swim together." The organization then is not successful unless—and until—everyone on the team is successful. That's a powerful culture!

If accountability to the mission and vision is lacking, the question to ask is, "Why?" The answers should point specifically to other pillars that need strengthening. When accountability is lacking, other pillars likely have visible cracks that need reinforcing.

Hiring Accountable People

Rather than encourage accountability *after hiring*, it's important to task the Human Resources department with bringing in individuals with a willingness to be accountable. It's up to HR to explain the mission and vision of the organization during interviews and determine if new hires can find their purpose there. For new hires to be consistently accountable requires two things.

First, they must be aligned with the organization's mission and strategy.

Second, they must be empowered to take appropriate action in pursuit of the vision and goals, while remaining anchored to the organization's core values.

Leaders of organizations must also remember that account-ability is not just about customers; it has a 360-degree scope that involves all stakeholders, including direct reports, peers, managers, business partners, suppliers, and society as a whole. When others experience the demonstration of accountability shown by a colleague, they, too, will be encouraged to be more accountable. This creates a virtuous spiral of success attributes such as passionate teamwork and innovation. A culture of accountability also prompts individuals to explore and exhibit personal leadership.

When Accountability is Missing

When accountability is missing, the attitude is one of, "I'm just doing my job and collecting my check." It doesn't matter to those individuals how their performance level affects the team, division, or organization. A perfect example of what happens when there is a lack of accountability is the Wells Fargo scandal that began in 2016. Decisions were made and actions were taken without consideration of the consequences. Many employees turned a blind eye to what transpired.

When individuals lack accountability, they put their heads down, go to work, collect their paychecks, and rarely look around them to consider how their actions impact others. Even when their personal work ethic is acceptable, they're not really team players, which can negatively impact alignment.

Employees who hold themselves accountable and are aligned around the mission and vision find it hard to accept misaligned behaviors. When you have a group of employees who are aligned, and someone else comes in who hasn't bought in, the organization will begin policing itself as to accountability, and there will be peer pressure to do the right thing.

In strongly aligned organizations, it is not enough for individuals to be accountable for their own work responsibilities. Everyone on the team becomes accountable to each other. Well-aligned organizations leverage their missions to provide a shared focus on goals and outcomes, and employees come together for a common purpose. They are more than willing to engage in an open exchange of ideas with each other and work to enhance the results for everyone. The result is that they provide tremendous value to each other, not just to the organization.

An example of personal, team, and joint accountability is demonstrated by football teams that make it to the Super Bowl each year—specifically with their offensive lines. Each member of the line has specific duties regarding their blocking assignments. Before and after the snap, they make adjustments to blocking schemes that transfer responsibility on the fly. When one lineman fails, the line fails, which means the overall offense fails.

Offensive lines consistently and intentionally practice together as well as with their teammates, including running backs, receivers, and quarterback. They do this to build up continuity, accountability, and alignment. They communicate back and forth. They watch films to discover weaknesses, not to point fingers, but to develop better strategies. They are accountable to each other and ultimately to the success of the whole team. Each lineman has complete confidence that the others will perform to a high level.

The Accountability Culture

We all know or have heard stories about individuals, whether in leadership positions or not, who seem unmotivated or fearful about making decisions. They fear making a misstep to such a high degree that they do little or nothing. Leaders need to help people with their level of commitment to the mission and to become accountable for their actions—good or bad. The question to ask is: "Are you motivated enough to do your job and do it well?" Managers and leaders who take the time to ask this question are often surprised by how many answer, "Yes." Yet, the motivation has not been obvious. In such instances, the leader may need to look at themselves and how they are leading. Are they really helping others to develop and grow through their positions? A leader can be accountable here by taking a hard look at whether the culture overly punishes mistakes or doesn't recognize and applaud efforts that may have ended in "failure" but brought about great learning opportunities.

Engaging the Quiet Ones

When some individuals receive a lack of attention or even ambivalence from their managers and leaders, they go silent. They withdraw. They stop caring. They believe the organization doesn't see their value. They are only accountable to themselves and their paychecks.

When someone has a strong skillset, yet doesn't draw attention to themselves, it's easy for them to become overlooked and underutilized. They may not be encouraged to demonstrate personal accountability or to join forces with others to engage in shared accountability. It is up to the leader to determine how to reach employees like these and put them in positions to succeed, even though they may not feel comfortable about touting their accomplishments or capabilities. It's up to the leaders to maximize their talents and skills to the benefit of the organization's stakeholders.

Collaboration and Accountability

In his book, *Lessons from Mars: How One Global Company Cracked the Code on High Performance Collaboration and Teamwork,* Carlos Valdes-Dapena shared that a team at Mars Inc. increased growth by 33% over one year after focusing efforts on collaboration in the workplace rather than on individual effort. He says, "The sense of accountability for their work together, based on agreements they forged, made their working relationships far more productive than they had been." It was discovered that to get people to work well together, it was best to let *them* figure out how to come up with solutions or improve results. When they were part of devising the solution, they were automatically accountable for it.

When Accountability is Lacking

When leaders recognize that the pillar of accountability is out of alignment, it's time to take a look at the possible causes. What are the factors that lead to a lack of personal accountability?

1. A culture where employees lack the means to have their voices heard and their ideas valued.

2. A lack of challenging work or options for improving how their job gets done.
3. Isolation. A lack of acceptance or engagement from other team members, managers, and leaders.
4. A lack of variety. Their jobs leave no room for developing or gaining new knowledge.
5. A somber environment. Lack of positive energy wears on people.
6. No clearly defined goals. Goals and objectives are not tied to the mission, nor are they communicated well or reviewed regularly.

All of these factors can and should be turned around by leaders. Begin by making changes at a high level. Get a personal commitment from all the leaders to change the culture and create a "shared accountability" pact. Communicate the concerted effort to improve the culture throughout the organization. Establish expectations around accountability and regularly enforce them. When personal or joint accountability is demonstrated, praise it in front of the group. Never be frugal with praise. What gets recognized gets repeated!

Leaders can have a significant impact on accountability simply by opening up the floor and listening to their teams. Be willing to hold yourself accountable. It can be daunting to put yourself in a position of receiving constructive feedback or criticism, but being open and humble is a high-level, emotionally intelligent state that will serve you well. As Maya Angelou was noted for saying, "Do the best you can until you know better. Then, when you know better, you do better."

Be willing to call out poor accountability and take proper action to correct it. Good leaders, however, don't just take corrective action. They look deeper to understand the potential causes that brought this situation to light. It's much better to look for the disease than to treat the symptoms. Be fair and consistent in these efforts. Highlight the proper actions that should have occurred and connect what was done to the organization's mission and vision.

Once baseline standards for personal and team accountability have been set, observe what happens. Have you cultivated the culture well enough? Are there some who are taking it on more effectively than others? Is the team policing themselves instead of you having to step into situations? Analyzing the results of efforts over time will enable you to build accountability up to the standard and then raise it appropriately.

Given consistent effort at encouraging accountability, you should see an improvement in alignment within this pillar fairly quickly. Communication within teams and across divisions will also increase because everyone is now accountable to the same mission. When a team's shared accountability strategies are executed smoothly, course corrections are made almost on autopilot. Not only does everyone play their roles as expected, but many willingly go the extra mile to reduce costs, delight customers, or do whatever it takes to enable the organization to do better.

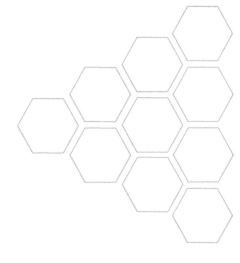

CHAPTER 9

EMPOWERMENT

"People want to be given responsibility to help solve the problem and the authority to act on it."
– Howard Schultz

Before leaders can empower others, there needs to be a clear understanding of what it means to do so. The term is often used in business yet is rarely defined. So, what is empowerment? It's an umbrella term that includes everything that enhances the capacity of employees to make good decisions and take positive actions that lead to desirable outcomes—without necessarily going to others for permission. Empowerment goes a long way toward eliminating bottlenecks in implementing strategic plans.

Empowerment is vital to workplace culture. Microsoft's Bill Gates has said, "As we look ahead, leaders will be those who empower others." The inference here is that empowering others (versus influencing followers) is the way of the future for leaders. Rather than *climbing* the corporate ladder, tomorrow's leaders will be *lifted up* into higher positions by those they empower to complete strategic plans.

Because a leader's role is to define the vision, create buy-in for it, and inspire people to work with passion to achieve it, the links between leadership, empowerment, and organizational success are tightly bound. Every organization relies collectively on its employees for success, but unless everyone is aligned with the mission and vision, the organization may struggle to succeed. Alignment means that employees know the organization's vision, strategies, and goals and how their individual roles contribute to these elements.

Eliminating the Rocks in the Road

Leaders and managers must seek out the impediments that keep work from flowing and strategic plans from being implemented. Those impediments might be policies, practices, organizational culture, or having people with the wrong skillsets in certain positions. Leaders must constantly be on the lookout for those rocks in the road and work to eliminate them. There will be times when employees can (and should be) given the authority to remove roadblocks without depending on leaders to make it happen. Employees who are working closely with customers or are deeply involved in an internal project may have greater insights than the leaders into what solutions are required. Frequent conversations between leaders, managers, and employees are critical to the evolution of empowerment. Every time managers meet with employees, the goal should be that the employees leave the meeting feeling empowered within their roles.

Research by the Gallup Organization[5] suggests that organizations that empower their employees to make decisions regarding customer needs experience 50 percent greater customer loyalty. This reduces the resources required to retain customers, freeing up those resources to gain new business, thus increasing profits. Effective use of empowerment can lead to a healthier bottom line.

Empowered teams can achieve tangible business results in any area of the company. Here are just a few examples of companies that benefited tremendously by empowering their employees:[6]

- At Johnson & Johnson, employees were empowered to come up with ways to reduce inventory levels. The result of strategies implemented was a $6 million per year reduction in inventory levels with no negative impact on customers.
- FedEx was able to cut service errors by 13 percent by empowering employees to come up with and implement solutions to service errors.
- At Yum! Brands (owner of KFC, Pizza Hut, Long John Silver's, A&W, and Taco Bell), every employee is empowered to make decisions on behalf of customers for up to $15. Many instances have been reported where discounts of $10 or free salads have been offered, resulting in customer appreciation, higher loyalty, repeat customers, and word-of-mouth praise.

To illustrate how empowerment works, let's assume that an airline's advertisements proclaim, "We go the extra mile for our customers." Now, imagine a situation where a passenger has missed his flight. At the check-in counter, as this passenger is attempting to book another flight, he is told by the agent that although there is a flight with seats available, the customer has to pay an additional fee to book because "that's what the rules say." The passenger would likely do so but not be happy about it.

Imagine what would have happened instead if the gate agent had been empowered by her superiors to "go the extra mile." The agent invites the passenger to board the flight without paying any additional fees. The delighted passenger later writes to the airline's CEO to express her gratitude, lauding the agent for adhering to the spirit of the airline's advertisements and becoming an advocate of the company when talking with friends and associates.

Via a company-wide email, the CEO acknowledges the agent's action as a shining example of alignment with the airline's vision. The agent is an empowered employee, and the CEO is a leader who knows the value of empowerment.

Despite numerous examples of the positive power of empowerment, many leaders are not comfortable empowering employees. They limit their employees' freedom to think and make decisions—effectively killing the benefit potential of real empowerment. Moreover, these leaders invest more time and effort in micromanaging, which negatively impacts morale and inhibits creativity. Such leaders don't understand the true power and impact of empowerment and how it can benefit the individual and organization. Entrepreneurial advisor Sharon Lechter understands the power in giving employees the reins when she says, "It doesn't make sense to hire smart people, then tell them what to do; we hire smart people so they can tell us what to do." When you hire people with unique skills and talents, let them use their gifts to the benefit of the organization!

Even Napoleon Bonaparte understood this. He is quoted as saying, "When I give a minister an order, I leave it to him to find the means to carry it out." That simple statement encapsulates an important truth about empowerment. Leaders must give their people a reasonable degree of freedom within the bounds of safety norms, morals, ethics, and compliance with laws to come up with their own ways of working toward agreed-upon objectives.

Helping Employees Take Calculated Risks

You can't just tell subordinates that they're "empowered" and expect them to behave that way. Successful empowerment is evidenced during interactions with employees. The goal for leaders is to give employees the confidence to take calculated risks. When employees do take risks and fail, it's important to avoid the "blame game." Rather, use those instances as additional learning opportunities.

When an employee takes independent action, and things don't go as expected, leaders may need to help the employee discover the lesson learned. Once again, rather than pointing out the error, strong leaders ask questions to help the employee find the answers. Examples of questions to consider are:

"Why did you make that decision?"

"What factors were considered?"

"How would you handle this situation differently if it were to arise again?"

Stay focused on the lesson learned and how to make better decisions in the future instead of taking power away by telling them what to do. By the way, this is an excellent way of helping children to learn life lessons, too.

In some highly regulated industries where great levels of bureaucracy are required, it's important to work with employees to understand the reasons behind the rules. Those rules serve as the boundaries of what can and cannot be done. It's also important to clarify which areas of employees' jobs do not fall under dictated rules and regulations. When employees know there are areas of their jobs where they can demonstrate personal discretion, that degree of empowerment helps boost accountability.

In highly aligned organizations, individuals have the autonomy they need to do their jobs without excessive oversight. Decision-making is done at the lowest possible level within the boundaries of established processes. While employees in organizations are held accountable and supported by others, they also have the authority to make decisions about how to do their jobs well. The organization is not handcuffed or overburdened with unnecessary policies or procedures that hold people back.

Organizations laden with bureaucracy or hierarchical management are full of frustrated employees. Their employees feel micromanaged and watched over, there is little autonomy in their work, and there is little trust in the leadership.

Overly Prescriptive Policies

Those in leadership of some organizations hesitate to empower individuals. Instead, they keep the power for themselves with overly prescriptive policies and a lack of transparency. That is a huge mistake because those leaders can quickly and easily become bottlenecks in the workflow as everyone awaits their answers to questions.

Instead of empowering people to think of the best answers on their own, these types of leaders rely on deeply detailed policies and procedures that figuratively tie employees' hands when it comes to responding quickly and effectively to both internal and external customers. Such constraints come across as not having confidence in people's abilities to think for themselves, which leads to poor morale, a lack of accountability, and interferes with teamwork.

A simple and light-hearted example of how a clear approach to empowerment works occurred in 2009 when Mary Barra was vice president of global human resources at General Motors. No less than 10 pages of the company's policies and procedures manual were attributed to the dress code. Barra felt it was time for the company culture to change around that topic. She changed the policy for the dress code to two words: "Dress appropriately."

When Barra received pushback from a manager worried about how his team would respond to this change—that they might dress too casually—she empowered him to speak with his team about what they deemed as "appropriate." Working together, his team came up with a plan for days when casual attire was appropriate and when something more professional was needed. Barra's opinion was that if the team could not handle defining "dress appropriately," they may struggle with much more important decisions. She is quoted as saying, "If you have overly prescriptive policies and procedures, people will live down to them. But if you let people own policies themselves, it aids their development as businesspeople."

Consider what happens when you don't foster a culture of empowerment. You will be bombarded daily for instruction on how to get the job done, which will interfere with your own job performance. When an employee asks for permission to do something, rather than giving it, empower them to come up with a good answer. When you immediately give a yes or no answer, instead of empowering employees to make decisions, you rob them of the opportunity to feel empowered. You become responsible for the result of the action taken, and the employee will likely continue to come to you for input on simple decisions.

Empowerment and Accountability Are Connected

It's important to note that leaders cannot expect accountability without giving empowerment. If individuals do not have the power to do what they need to do to get the job done, they cannot be held accountable for the results. The whole idea of empowerment is for leaders to push decision-making down to those closest to the problem. When the right people are hired for positions within the company, they should not require heavy oversight. Once they've been trained and given the proper tools to be successful, they should be empowered to make decisions around the results expected of them.

Think back to the Nordstrom example in the section on accountability. Nordstrom employees are empowered to satisfy their customers on the spot. When Nordstrom implemented this policy, the feedback from customers was better than expected. Nordstrom's value, in the eyes of its customers, went sky-high, and other companies wanted to emulate "The Nordstrom Experience."

How to Empower Others

To empower individuals, teams, and divisions, stop doing their jobs for them! Even if you know the answer to their question and can handle it quickly, you're only making others dependent on you for their actions. When you instead invest a few moments to ask their opinion and help them make the best decision, they become empowered and will make better decisions going forward. Here's a super simplified dialogue to consider the next time you are asked for a solution or permission from an employee you want to empower.

Employee: *Are you OK with me doing* _____?
Leader: *Is it within your job description to do it?*
Employee: *Yes.*

Leader: *OK. It's within your job description, and since I have you in that role, I have all the trust and confidence that you'll make the right decision.*

If the employee hesitates, continue with:
Leader: *Are you not closer to this situation than I am?*
Employee: *Yes.*
Leader: *Then what's keeping you from making the decision?*
Employee: *I just wanted to make sure it's alright with you.*
Leader: *Have you considered other options?*
Employee: *Yes.*
Leader: *Let's hear them.*
Encourage the employee to explain their thinking.
Leader: *Which option did you like best, and what's keeping you from implementing it? Is it something I said, or a challenge within the organization?*

That is how you help empowered employees gain confidence in their decision-making abilities. When their explanation for their choice is sound, you simply agree and point out the good decision made. Probing an employee's logic and reasoning in this way not only creates empowerment but will also likely lead to a better decision. If there are obstacles in the way, it's your job as a leader to remove them. However, the decision on which action to take remains theirs. They own it. They also "own" the praise that is earned for accomplishing the goal.

When employees are recognized for following orders or directives, the recognition is not really for that person, is it? It's for the directives and orders and those who created them. The person involved only did what they were told to do. On the other hand, recognition for those who've been empowered to make thoughtful and useful decisions on their own is truly noteworthy.

Bill George, former CEO of Medtronic, and leadership expert Peter Sims say, "The most empowering condition of all is when the entire organization is aligned with its mission, and people's passions and purpose are in sync with each other."

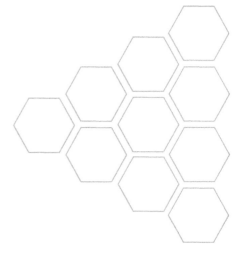

CHAPTER 10

TEAMWORK

"Teamwork is the ability to work together toward a common vision. The ability to direct individual accomplishments toward organizational objectives. It is the fuel that allows common people to attain uncommon results."
– Andrew Carnegie

Teamwork starts at the top. Leaders who demonstrate effective teamwork set an example for everyone else in the organization. To evaluate the level of teamwork at any level, ask these questions:

1. How well do we work as a team? Are we in agreement on the clarity of the mission and vision? Are we in agreement about the messaging that will be directed longitudinally?

2. How well do we work together across departments? Is everyone working in the best interest of the mission and vision of the organization?

3. What would be the ideal state of teamwork within the organization? How do we compare with that ideal at this point in time?

Aligned organizations rely on the ability of both leaders and employees to work collaboratively on common goals. This includes having employees who are not afraid to reach out to colleagues or outside resources for help. Everyone in the organization understands how their collective work connects with the mission and vision and work. They work together to make certain they are aligned to that purpose.

Great teams are able to accomplish more together than the sum of their individual work. The goal is to create synergy within the collective. When that happens, it is likely that organizations can do more with less. So, how do we get an organization to achieve more with fewer resources? The short answer is alignment. Teamwork represents an organization's expression of alignment. Teams that have a shared, common goal with KPI progress points communicate that progress well and express success through effective recognition.

A candid and complete evaluation of leadership effectiveness would include an assessment of teamwork. Let's assume that your team has a low teamwork score, which suggests that people believe they are mostly working on their own. While they may do their jobs effectively, they may not think of themselves as being part of a team with a common vision. When this is the case, the team leader is likely ineffective at pulling the group together. As a result, the team members may be managing tasks rather than focusing on results. The big picture is one where these team members are not exerting effort to change the beliefs and experiences of others to see the reasoning behind working together and holding one another accountable.

Those with low scores in teamwork may believe their group works well together and that they like each other, but these team members are not working with the overall organization's purpose in mind. While these team members have been putting in the minimum requirements necessary to function in their roles, they're likely not exceeding that minimum or working collaboratively to achieve desired results. We call that not playing at "game speed." It's also likely that these employees do not interact effectively with other departments or divisions.

The Silo Effect

Many organizations, divisions, and departments are naturally siloed based on their organization and/or operations. For example, the chemistry faculty in a high school would be considered "siloed," in the sense that their curriculum pertains primarily to the instruction of chemistry. That part is fine, as specific work needs to be done within a dedicated structure and process. Expertise sometimes needs to be concentrated for the benefit of the organization.

However, silos in organizations become an operational impediment when members of the silo do not consistently share information, goals, tools, priorities, and processes with others. This "silo mentality" can negatively impact operations, reduce employee morale, and contribute to the overall failure of a company. Members of various silos derive their power and status from the group—their tribe. They think alike and will likely work at a similar level of engagement—not necessarily in alignment.

Identifying and remedying unhealthy silos is critical to achieving organizational alignment. For example, the Anoka County (Minnesota) Sheriff's Department discovered that there wasn't enough understanding and appreciation of how the actions taken in various departments affected other departments. Those on patrol weren't well-versed in the work done by investigators or evidence technicians to ensure casework was brought to fruition. While there wasn't time available to cross-train members of the various teams, time *was* carved out for various employees to come alongside those in other areas of the department and report back. These efforts led to greater collaboration and consideration of the effort across the departments. It has also led to better evidence handling and process improvements that allow them to serve their citizens more transparently.

As with any change-related effort, acknowledging and identifying the problem must come first. In this instance, it means stating that silos sometimes exist to protect assets or data—but mostly for vertical and functional synergy. They're unhealthy to organizations and need to be changed before alignment can be achieved.

Here are the symptoms of silo mentality:

1. Creativity is hindered
2. Cronyism sets in

3. Best practices are not leveraged or shared
4. Productivity has peaks and valleys
5. Star performers become disgruntled and may leave.

The silo effect is common in many corporations. For example, let's look at how a typical vice president of finance might operate. While this vice president may excel at overseeing and fulfilling finance department operations, she may stumble when asked to collaborate with other departments such as marketing. Leaders of those diverse departments have very different mindsets and skillsets. One operates from the left side of the brain, the other from the right. So, the relationship often begins with a disconnect.

The vice president of finance is not likely to understand the rationale behind the projections from the vice president of marketing. Meanwhile, the vice president of marketing understands that when a new product is being launched in a new marketplace, there are limitations as to how well projections can be made until there's experience.

If finance and marketing are not aligned to the mission, it could negatively impact the organization's ability to forecast and budget effectively. Furthermore, when there is no alignment between finance and marketing, the ground is fertile for infighting and one-upmanship. This may be compounded when leaders of these departments are both "A-players" who are trying to achieve higher status within the organization.

Does this type of scenario sound familiar? If a team's leaders are more focused on looking good to their superiors, they will likely negatively affect the organization overall, and everyone suffers as a result. Eliminating this situation may require intervention by someone higher up the organization or requiring each party to shadow the other for an allotted time to gain a better understanding of how they operate and why.

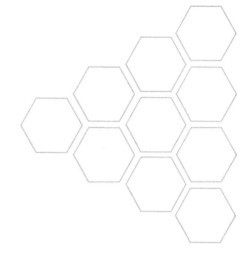

CHAPTER 11

CREATIVITY

"A business has to be involving, it has to be fun,
and it has to exercise your creative instincts."
– Richard Branson

ew ideas are a lifeline for organizations to enable long-term, sustainable growth. Employees who are in the trenches every day, interacting with customers and stakeholders, regularly talk about things that are not working and what they'd like to see changed. Sadly, few organizations put processes in place for such discussions, which lead to innovation. They just don't include the need for creativity in their organizational plans.

Aligned organizations promote and value idea generation. They create opportunities for employees to not only develop, but to share their ideas. All employee ideas are welcomed and leveraged to improve the organization.

A great example of this type of approach is with a business training company. The company set a goal of lowering overhead, requesting ideas from every department and employee. Everyone was empowered to look at their own processes, teams, and departments, but their input was not limited. They were encouraged to ask questions of those in other departments, too. No idea was too small to be considered, and questions about the efficiency of procedures were welcome. A time period was set for ideas to be submitted, and all of the ideas were compiled and shared with the entire company. The benefit of doing this was that when employees saw others' ideas, more ideas came to mind. What was really interesting was that some of the ideas related to purchasing didn't originate with the purchasing department— they came from the shipping department! One idea alone generated a 30 percent savings in the cost of inventory.

Creativity is the catalyst for innovation within organizations. When leaders encourage open communications, the likelihood of coming up with impactful ideas increases. Creating a repository of ideas shared throughout leadership teams allows specific actions to be analyzed and processes to be changed for the better. Empowerment also begets creativity. An employee who is empowered to make certain decisions may, in the course of accomplishing that goal, find a new and novel way of getting at a problem or opportunity. As long as ideas are shared (whether they prove fruitful or not), the team and the organization benefit. Those ideas can spur other ideas, as well as foster the mindset that ideas, in general, are encouraged.

When Creativity is Lacking

When creativity is lacking in an organization, it's time to determine if it's a mission, leadership, process, or employee issue.

- **A Mission Issue**: If your organization doesn't espouse continuous learning and improvement, it's tough to operationalize creativity. Take a look at how creativity is being encouraged in key initiatives, strategies, and programs. If creativity is lacking or stifled, it's time to take a look at how it can be implemented.

- **A Leadership Issue**: When key executives don't hold teams accountable for creating processes that encourage new ideas, it just won't happen. You get the results you're structured to get. When leaders set an example of constantly seeking out new and creative ways of improving the organization, everyone takes note.

- **A Process Issue:** At first, most ideas are just skeletons of what they could eventually become. Broader considerations might make them implausible. That doesn't mean an idea is bad. That idea should still be captured and considered as something that could become more substantive. When ideas are not given proper due, they wither away. A great way to help the creative process at the early stage is to encourage the person who generated the idea to further explore other factors that might help. This can be a development opportunity for employees to expand beyond their "set" roles.

- **An Employee Issue:** This is rarely the case unless you have hired people who thrive on being told what to do. If you have, it's time for a change. First, establish a culture of openness to ideas. Encourage individuals and teams to flesh out ideas, and you will find the organization a recipient of many more. Ask questions like:

"How does the idea fit in with our mission, vision, or strategic plan?"

"What do you see as the process to make this idea come to life?"

"Who do you think would need to be involved?"

"What might the cost or revenue implications be?"

When you have a system in place for taking in ideas and appreciation is expressed for them, the line of communication becomes truly bi-directional, and the benefits increase exponentially.

Creativity as a Team Effort

When team members make contributions that end up in new strategic plans, they cannot help but buy into them. Wise leaders recognize the ideas, work to develop strategies for implementing them, and take those plans back down the line for refinement before presenting them to the broader organization. Organizations operating with openness to creativity generate more robust and innovative ideas than those in which new ideas are not valued.

When the term "creativity" is mentioned in the context of business, many leaders equate it with the term "innovation." What comes to mind are companies like Apple, Google, Salesforce, Tesla, Amazon, and Netflix. These companies have publicly demonstrated creativity in remaining relevant to their customers.

But organizational creativity is not just about high-profile innovations that lead to industry-disrupting products like iTunes, nor is it the preserve of the company's research and development teams. Harnessing employee creativity can be useful even if it is not widely seen by the outside world or results only in incremental changes to the way the organization is run.

- In the 1980s, American Airlines reported saving $100,000 a year by reducing just one olive from each salad served on its flights. That suggestion came from within.
- More recently, Xerox asked its employees to "adopt a living plant" in the organization and take responsibility for watering it. By eliminating the need for an external service provider to tend to the plants, the company saved $200,000 a year.

Nearly every company talks about how it delivers "innovative solutions" for its customers or how good it is at tapping its employees' "creativity." Yet not many companies are truly able to channel the creative energies of their employees to improve operational excellence, product ideas, or customer experience.

The Suggestion Box is Not Where Ideas Go to Die

What most often limits employee creativity is the lack of a suitable mechanism that allows them to express that creativity. Some organizations have a suggestion box type of system for employees to share ideas, but, often, the ideas stop there. No one is charged with analyzing the ideas and getting back to those who suggested them. If the idea is not feasible, wise leaders at least acknowledge the individual for trying and encourage them to try again. With bi-directional communication between the idea's creator and the person or team reviewing ideas, it could be that other, better ideas are created. The suggestion box should not be where ideas go to die. When that happens, employees adopt a "why bother" attitude and stop sharing their ideas.

One of the foundational reasons for low creativity in an organization is simple: People are afraid of rejection. They fear that their ideas may not be considered seriously or that an ill-conceived idea could be career-limiting. Organizations that consistently deliver superior performance create and sustain a culture that nurtures creativity and learning by eliminating this fear. During meetings, employees are encouraged to share their thoughts on issues or to harness opportunities. Their leaders listen, devoting time and energy to studying ideas and suggestions put forward by employees. Leaders are motivated to implement new ideas, and more importantly, reward and recognize employees whose ideas are adopted. This not only motivates the employees who demonstrated creativity but also ignites a passion in others to unleash their own creative potentials.

While it is true that not all ideas that bubble up will be workable, organizations that listen to their employees are able to energize them by signaling that they value divergent thinking. Ideas that may not work in their specific context may spur on other ideas when put in front of a different lens. This requires a degree of openness in the organization's leaders and managers—they must be willing to set aside their personal prejudices and other baggage to listen to ideas from employees without pre-judging them. They need to broaden their perspectives to see the possibilities outside of their normal view. Leaders encourage employees to follow through with implementing their ideas and give them the necessary resources to make it happen.

Organizations whose leaders lead through fear and intimidation will always lack creativity. Employees will feel inhibited and unable to express their creativity. In turn, this will lead to dissatisfaction and higher attrition.

Raising the Level of Creativity

What does it take to raise the level of employee creativity in an organization? Leaders need to foster bi-directional communication and ensure that employees are aligned with their vision, mission, and values. Author Bob Sutton says, "At places where intense innovation happens, they often combine people who know a little with people who know too much. The tension between massive knowledge and fresh thinking can spark a fundamental breakthrough."

Too often, organizations rely on the same people over and over for innovation. They bring in those who are perceived to have the best knowledge of product development or internal processes to make new decisions. The challenge with this kind of approach is that many of these folks arrive with pre-conceived notions, baggage, and blinders. Strong leaders don't hesitate to mix up the players when innovation is needed. People who know a little, but not enough to be dangerous, often come into creative meetings with fresh perspectives and different experiences that can take ideas in new and different directions.

Before creating a team that is blended with experts and non-experts, there are two things to take into consideration:

1. For those who know just a little about the issue at hand, make certain they understand their role in the process and are comfortable speaking their mind in front of those with a greater level of expertise and experience.
2. Set the stage for the culture of this type of session. Put a non-judgmental facilitator or moderator in place to ensure roles, ideas, and opinions are valued and appreciated.

It may be challenging for the "experts" to be questioned by those who only know a little about the topic at hand. However, when your experts are willing and able to humble themselves to be open to the comments, questions, and ideas that come forth, they may be pleasantly surprised at how they can use their expertise in new ways. This can prove to be a quite fulfilling and educational experience for those experts. Know that not every mix will prove fruitful, but without it, creativity will definitely be limited.

Frances Arnold was a co-recipient of a 2018 Nobel Prize in chemistry. One of the most interesting things about this is that Ms. Arnold is not a chemist—she has training as a mechanical engineer! She acknowledged that her training allowed her to "be able to look at the problem with a fresh set of eyes," realizing that, "The way most people were going about protein engineering was doomed to failure."[7] She was able to apply her knowledge from a different discipline to a problem that wasn't getting solved through traditional methods within that field. The end result was the creation of a best practice for creating a transformational new process that enables people to develop revolutionary products to help others.

You may believe the chances of your organization doing something Nobel-worthy are slim. Within the constructs of the areas in which the Nobel Prize is given, that may be true. However, when "Nobel-worthy" is defined as coming up with ideas and processes that can transform how your organization serves both its internal and external customers, it's a winning proposition.

Once you have a process in place that encourages creativity, employees will feel empowered, connected with leadership, and more engaged in teamwork. Even when the ideas that come of the process aren't all that promising, the results of the process will bring tangential benefits.

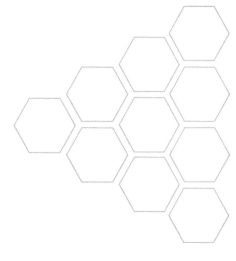

CHAPTER 12

BEST PRACTICES

"Excellence is the gradual result
of always striving to do better."
– Pat Riley

Best practices are defined as commercial or professional procedures that are accepted or prescribed as being correct or most effective. Aligned organizations actively seek out and share best practices throughout the organization. They encourage all employees from the leadership down to look outside the organization—even outside the industry—for better ways to do their work. They maintain a learning mindset and are OK with admitting, "We do not have all the answers." Input from others is never overlooked or ignored.

Finding and implementing best practices requires a deliberate process, but the process must also be consistent. Practices are benchmarked and regularly measured for areas of improvement. Everyone in the organization should have a mindset of asking questions such as:

"Is this the best way to do this?"

"Are we as efficient as we can be?"

"Are we providing all of the benefits the customers expect from us?"

"What more could we do?"

In this manner, best practices are strongly connected with creativity.

When Best Practices Are Non-Existent

When best practices—or, at least, a path of growth and learning *toward* best practices—are not put in place or adhered to, everyone's experience with the organization is diminished. This includes everyone from the leadership teams down to individuals and, ultimately, customers. Teams and divisions become insulated and lack sufficient input on new ideas. The business as a whole becomes resistant to change or even unaware of new ways of thinking and working. Simply put, businesses that do not implement best practices fail.

When Best Practices Are Encouraged

When discovering best practices becomes a common goal, the organization opens the eyes and ears of every individual to seek ways of improving everything from their own jobs to how the organization is perceived in the marketplace.

- The leadership of Medtronic discovered its practice of marketing designed to appeal to patients by looking outside its industry to the pharmaceutical field. When Medtronic began appealing directly to patients and making them more aware of their products and solutions, it prompted patients to directly request that their doctors use Medtronic products.

- When IBM's personal computer company was losing market share to Hewlett Packard, evaluating HP's practices enlightened IBM to the untapped potential of a declining market—personal use printers and supplies. Lexmark was launched using best practices gleaned from the competition.

- Stephens County School District (Georgia) achieved high test scores by improving efforts at all levels. This was accomplished simply by communicating the mission and vision regularly and deliberately throughout the district. When leadership shares stories of how the mission is being carried out, people better understand how they can connect with it and help others in the district do the same.

Best practices are meant to be applied to all areas of the organization, from the development of strategies, to data collection and distribution, to compensation and recognition programs, to talent management and the allocation of resources. If an organization is not open to *implementing* best practices in all areas, it can be hard to encourage best practice recommendations. When new and improved practices are put in place, that information should be shared throughout the organization to encourage even more feedback. Employees need to feel empowered to develop and suggest best practices as well as to implement them.

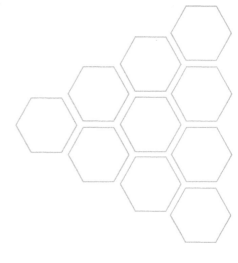

CHAPTER 13

DEVELOPMENT

"Technology is nothing. What's important is that you have a faith in people, that they're basically good and smart, and if you give them tools, they'll do wonderful things with them."
– Steve Jobs

Modern-day philosopher Jim Rohn was noted for his wit and wisdom. He was a strong proponent of the training and development of employees. Once an audience member asked, "What if I train them and they leave?" Jim's reply was, "What if you don't train them and they stay?"

Forward-thinking organizations have plans and budgets in place for employee development. They recognize that good employees seek opportunities to grow and develop within their jobs and careers. Aligned organizations go beyond job-specific training to offering all levels of employees the opportunity to develop not just job skills but management and leadership competencies.

By developing managers who can coach and provide career guidance to others, everyone benefits—the employees *and* the company. These companies embrace and champion continual learning as a key strategic lever for success. Even if these employees don't progress to leadership levels, the skills and traits they've taken on through development will likely help them, their teams, and the organization perform at a higher level. Development impacts many alignment constructs, including creativity, empowerment, best practices, and communication.

In less-aligned organizations, training options might be available but are not required or necessarily supported. Those with little or no dedication to development may outwardly frown on employees "taking time off" to attend seminars or training sessions, as if their absence is a hardship on those who do not choose to develop themselves. In these types of companies, discussions about career goals are rare. When organizations don't provide employees time for development, they discourage employees from creatively exploring new possibilities for growth and improvement of processes. They merely see employees as inputs to provide specific outputs. When organizations don't value development, they typically also have weaknesses in their pillars of creativity and best practices.

Employees who are dedicated to developing themselves usually seek four things:

1. The best tools necessary to be effective in their positions.
2. Skills that apply not only to their current position but also add value to their overall careers.
3. Ways of seeing and/or contributing to issues and opportunities within other departments of the organization, which broadens their ability to make an impact.
4. Pay and recognition commensurate with the benefits delivered to the organization.

People will give the organization their best work, but they want to be self-actualized. This is a scenario where employees are saying, "I'll give you my best work, but I want you to help me round out my resume with additional skills training so if the organization goes through a down-sizing and I need another job, I've got the skills to land on my feet." This type of thinking references the Law of Reciprocity. That law states that when someone does something nice for you, you will have a deep-rooted psychological urge to do something nice in return. When all four of the above occur, employees will do even more for the organization to receive more benefits for themselves. This scenario creates a positive cycle of reciprocity that benefits all stakeholders and reduces burnout.

Forward-thinking organizations are on board with this. As an example, according to its *Career Choice* web page, Amazon will pay for 95 percent of tuition, fees, and textbooks—up to $12,000 over four years—for hourly associates with one year of tenure to earn "certificates and associate degrees in high-demand occupations such as aircraft mechanics, computer-aided design, machine tool technologies, medical lab technologies and nursing."[8]

Starbucks is another company that encourages development. Starbucks offers eligible partners the opportunity to earn a bachelor's degree with 100% tuition coverage, coaching, counseling, and advising through Arizona State University's top-ranked online degree programs.

It's important to note that reciprocity in business is also not a one-to-one proposition. Leaders will not—and don't—have time to recognize and praise every little thing an employee does right. There may be a culmination of actions necessary before acknowledgment occurs.

One way that leaders can be more appreciative of employee efforts is to acknowledge how the mundane, day-to-day work that's done by various people that binds a team together or allows others to do their job is as critically important as the work that is out in front of the world. Companies like UPS and FedEx have a structure where leaders truly understand the incredible value that truck loaders and unloaders bring to the organization and their customers because they, more often than not, started in that same role. Loading and unloading trucks is a thankless job, but without those people, neither of these companies could exist. Those loaders know when leaders come in to recognize them, they mean it because they were in the trenches themselves.

With a culture intent on appreciation and employee development, as well as a quantity and quality of tools provided to leaders, managers, and individuals, overall employee and organizational effectiveness will increase dramatically. With plenty of both quality and quantity, it only makes sense that the organization will be justified in having higher expectations of performance. Organizations that have lower standards regarding the tools they provide cannot expect high performance. That would be like expecting a ditch digger to use a shovel to dig the Panama Canal.

Development is a give-and-take situation. When organizations offer skill development, most employees will logically give their best work in return. These employees will be appreciative of opportunities to contribute and grow with the organization. Yet, in exchange for the organization's expectation of high performance, the worker expects to have development opportunities to meet and exceed those expectations.

Solid development opportunities also rest on the leader to implement. Leaders need to know each employee well enough to understand their skills, capabilities, needs, and experiences, and connect them with what might be available within the company. For example, a person who has done a great job of streamlining processes in her own department could be made available to look at how things get done in other departments. That employee may not see that kind of opportunity, but her leader should.

In lesser-aligned organizations, only the "squeaky wheels"—those who regularly request development opportunities for themselves—are likely to have opportunities to improve their skills. More reserved employees will be too uncomfortable to have conversations about their own skill training, development, advancement, and career-building. This lack of initiative and self-awareness will be reflected in their work. It's summed up in the adage, "I will do for you what you do for me." When leaders do not recognize or address this type of situation, shy employees may not contribute on an optimal level. Not all employees want to matriculate into higher-level positions, but most employees want to do a good job, and it's the responsibility of leadership to provide development opportunities to maximize their skills.

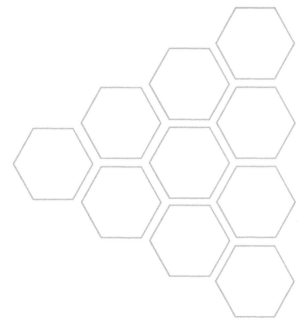

PART 3

THE DATA-DRIVEN
LEADERSHIP PLAYBOOK

CHAPTER 14

THE CRESCENDO EFFECT

When everyone in the organization performs at their best, teams operate "on all cylinders" and the business, as a whole, functions at peak capacity. That escalation in effort generates an upward spiral of intense focus and high performance. When that happens, a crescendo effect is created within the company to the benefit of all. The organization functions well, the employees work with passion and purpose, the customers benefit from products and services, and the shareholders receive a healthy return on their investment. It's the ultimate goal of every company.

The achievement of optimal operational flow can only happen when alignment occurs. Alignment is created through the strength of harmony between strategy, structure, and culture. With harmony between those three elements, linkages and synergies develop within teams and divisions, as well as between departments. Everyone understands the organization's goal, has the best tools available to perform their roles, and communication flows like spring water, nourishing everything it touches.

Leaders who dedicate themselves to developing such companies must first develop specific skills within themselves. Remember, great leaders work hard on themselves before asking others to give their all to the organization. Skills leaders must have in order to create alignment within their companies are:

1. The ability to synchronize macro data and boil it down to the individual contributor level in a manner that spawns role clarity.

2. A unique blend of foresight and keen understanding of human dynamics that facilitates hierarchal and functional optimization.

3. The uncanny capability to convey a message that establishes the purpose of the organization's existence in a manner that mitigates attenuation and creates a common set of beliefs that inspire appropriate action. Examples of the types of leaders who have succeeded at this are W. Edwards Deming, Warren Buffet, and Nelson Mandela.

These are not necessarily *technical* skills, but abilities to do the alignment work needed to get the organization humming. Alignment is achievable yet can be challenging to maintain. Anticipatory and perceptive leaders can identify when the alignment crescendo starts to dissipate and, like a conductor, begin building for the next one. This leadership skill compares to that of symphony conductors.

Have you ever noticed that conductors make gestures *before* the music changes? Or that they give cues to help musicians join in at just the right time and pace? That's because conductors are always a step ahead. They need to be a step ahead because it's their role to ensure that the orchestra plays the music as well as possible.

In any given piece, the conductor is "managing" the pacing and cohesion of up to 100 musicians, all having to work together, all following that lone person standing on the podium between the audience and the orchestra. That person's role is to keep all the musicians working in perfect unison for every second of the performance.

The conductor helps to shape the music by combining the composer's work with their own interpretation of it. Through this process, they help the musicians give life to the notes on the page, and the audience is able to enjoy and appreciate the resulting performance. The conductor is perhaps the perfect model for what it takes to be a great leader, manager, and facilitator. They have their fingers on the pulse of the orchestra as a whole and guide the musicians to execute their vision.

Just as a conductor "speaks" the language of music, leaders must speak the language of those they are trying to engage. When leaders truly understand what the individuals are trying to accomplish through their roles and skillsets, those leaders are able to use the correct language to tie the individuals' commitment and purpose to the goal of the organization and elevate the intensity of the performance. That's euphoria for an organization. Just as with a symphony, there is time to relish and delight in exceptional performance, but after the accolades and applause, everyone turns the page to prepare for the next performance. In business, after a crescendo is reached and appreciated, everyone knows they must build to the next one.

Structure That Leads to Crescendo

How do organizations achieve this crescendo effect? When considering the structure of an organization, questions such as these are asked and answered:

- Do we have people with the right skills in leadership roles?
- Do we have people with the right skills on our teams?
- Are we structured in a way to maximize the capabilities of the people within the organization? If not, do we change our people or our structure?

Changing the structure could involve a change in leadership or a shift in philosophy. However, a shift in philosophy could require a modification or re-prioritization of corporate values and is not to be considered lightly.

A structural change for the better might simply entail putting names in different boxes on the organizational chart. It could be that the chart itself needs to be rearranged. The important issue is to be able to utilize the skillsets of all the players at their maximum levels.

The best leaders invest the time and effort to understand the players on their teams and within their organizations. They learn peoples' skills, their roles, and their reaction styles to different stressors. They also learn of the individuals' expectation levels and what excites them as it relates to their work. Leaders must work at effectively recognizing and reflecting the value each person brings to the organization. When that is done well, foundations are built that employees respond to in a manner consistent with their hopes and expectations.

Strategy That Leads to Crescendo

How do leaders get employees to do what needs to be done in the best manner possible? How do they get the full buy-in of the team? What must leaders do and say for everyone to feel they play an important part in the strategy and its execution? How can leaders clarify each person's role and responsibilities?

This is where strategy comes into play. When those who are expected to implement a strategy have a say in its development, the execution level is greater. When expectations are clear, people take ownership. They understand that the organization is playing to their strengths, as their roles are outlined. They also know what roles others play as they relate to the strength of the strategy. And, the team members take ownership and pride in their part of the plan.

A perfect example of strategy and buy-in occurred within the great Chicago Bulls basketball team of the 1990s when Michael Jordan and Dennis Rodman were key players. Jordan's skill was in making the shots, and Rodman was unmatched in the NBA as a rebounder. Jordan knew that if Rodman got the rebound, the ball was coming his way. Rodman was not going to dribble the ball from one end of the floor to the other to attempt a three-point shot. His role and responsibility were to get that rebound securely and get it in the hands of someone who was going to score. The Bulls won three NBA championship titles with this type of team-first approach.

When it comes to implementing strategy, leaders should constantly ask themselves these questions:

1. What structure would drive optimal efficiency and productivity?
2. Are the right people in the right roles?
3. How aligned is our team, and how well are we performing against our strategic plan?
4. Am I contributing to or deterring a culture that imbues our mission and vision?

When we bring all these elements into alignment, an environment is created in which employees get excited around the success of the organization. People proactively share what they are doing. They get thrilled about "really doing this thing right," and the inevitable positive results that follow: a crescendo that punctuates collective success.

When Resilience is Tested

When speed, pressure, and workloads are ramped up toward the goal of peak performance, there will be opportunities for breakdowns, gaps, and miscommunication. Just like a faulty tire, the potential for serious damage increases with speed. With added pressure, gaps in alignment can worsen, causing a derailment in performance. This is where the leaders' skills listed above come into play.

In sports, this is likened to the difference between pre-season games, regular season games, and the playoffs. The pre-season is a time of testing skills, whether people are in the right roles, and if planned strategies need adjustment. The regular season is where the strategy, structure, and culture come together for the long haul. Areas of weakness will be discovered in games against more talented teams. The playoffs are where resilience is tested. As the pressure or pace demanded of higher expectations builds, resilience can and will wear down. However, it is the alignment of that team and its mental and emotional capability to respond to the pressure and attacks on their resiliency that plays the biggest factor in who wins.

How can organizational teams stay calm, understand situational factors, and then execute smoothly to achieve a crescendo of performance when the pressure's on?

There first needs to be an understanding that this is an iterative process. As an organization becomes more aligned, it will perform better at the pace and intensity that becomes the norm. However, as the pace ratchets up with the development of new products or the implementation of new strategic plans, areas of low resiliency are likely to be revealed. These weaknesses might be a result of:

- Individuals not being adaptive enough to handle new projects or roles. This is related to the structure of the organization. Adjustments may need to be made to help those individuals adapt, additional resources might need to be provided, or people may need to be moved into different roles.
- Some people may not have the technical skills in their roles to handle the workload. This is a development issue within

the structure of the organization. Added training may be required.

- The structure of the department or organization may be limiting. It may come to light that some evolutionary changes are required to maintain and build upon the momentum necessary to achieve the goal. This might involve changing leadership, bringing on new talent, rearranging roles attached to the goal, or even adjusting the philosophy of how the organization will get from point B to point C in terms of products, channels, and so on. This relates to the culture of an organization and speaks to continuous improvement.

How an organization responds to pressure is an inflection point where both leaders and individuals need to assess how they can build themselves up to be able to handle that next level of intensity. How can they increase their resiliency, talent level, and/or philosophy to enable them to get past that barrier? It's the leader's responsibility to make the right foundational and tactical decisions after thorough analysis.

When Change is Indicated

When the leadership of an organization agrees that changes are required in order to enhance performance, there are several things to take into consideration.

1. Are the changes being considered really going to resolve the challenge? A visual representation of this would be rearranging deck chairs on the Titanic. When that happens, *strategic* problems are being addressed with *structural* solutions. For example, when leaders choose to put different names in dif-

ferent boxes on the organizational chart, they may not be addressing something that's really a structural problem.

2. Is a culture of cronyism being put forth? Are the changes being considered in the best interest of the organization's mission and vision? Cronyism does little more than compound a *cultural* problem with a *structural* diversion.

3. Are changes being made for the sake of change? This is typically an ego play to shake things up, yet ends up creating an interruption of workflow and distraction within the organization. Many leaders think employees are unaware of their sleight of hand intentions. This is simply not true.

4. Is the potential of the organization being maximized to lead to a crescendo by playing to everyone's strengths—getting the right people into the right roles? When the right people are in the right roles, the team gets better because they believe in where they want to go and what they could be. They are more aligned in purpose and feel they have a good handle on the expectations to persevere against the intensity they couldn't overcome previously. Transparency, consistency, and adherence to the plan build trust. Trust mitigates message distortion, which contributes significantly to building that crescendo.

When all of these considerations are tended to, change is more widely accepted. Changes enhance workflow instead of disrupting it. Resiliency is increased, and the push toward the next crescendo is met with enthusiasm.

The crescendo effect happens as an organization becomes more capable at various levels due to the implementation of necessary changes. Everyone adjusts to handle increased pressure, expectations, and pace to the point where they perform at the highest levels. As performance improves, confidence is enhanced, and rally cries grow louder. This is when teams, divisions, and organizations *achieve* crescendo.

Monitoring While Building Toward Crescendo

When you're in the process of building to a crescendo, it's tremendously valuable to get a quick win. A quick win in a relatively short time frame heightens momentum. Conductors know that when and how well a certain chord is struck is an indicator of the success of the entire performance—how well-aligned each member of the orchestra is. It points toward a successful crescendo. Leaders in a corporate setting watch for indicators of alignment and point out those "quick wins" to all stakeholders. Quick wins in business could be defined as:

1. Quarter over quarter performance
2. Organizational growth versus industry growth
3. A sales uptick
4. Hitting benchmarks ahead of schedule

Uncovering the reasons performance improved and celebrating and recognizing these types of achievement goes a long way toward building momentum toward an organizational crescendo.

With proper analysis of teamwork and existing silos coupled with supporting data, systemic organizational challenges can be identified. Once the problem is framed appropriately, the solution can be an exciting exercise across the department through teamwork.

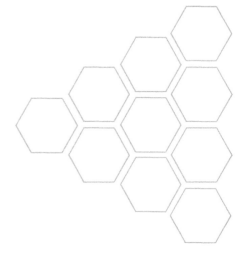

CHAPTER 15

THE PARADOX OF THE SMART PERSON

E ach person has areas of strength. When someone has specific expertise or knowledge about something, others will look at them as smarter and more capable than others. And, they may be smarter within that realm. The challenge arises when it is assumed that person will be just as capable in *other* areas.

Too often in business, the person who has demonstrated great capability on a team or within a department will be promoted into a leadership position. The assumption is that if they're so good at X, they should be able to lead others to be good at it, too. A perfect example of this is promoting the top salesperson to the position of sales manager without first evaluating their management skills. If they're not ready to take on a leadership position, the error in going through with this promotion is twofold:

1. The sales leader manages poorly.
2. The company risks losing the revenue generated by him or her as the top salesperson.

Time and again, we hear stories of smart people getting promoted and either not being happy in the new position or not excelling in it. When that happens, they've likely been promoted to the point of incompetence. This is not to say these people are incompetent in general, rather that they don't have the competency to excel in the new position. This is known as "The Peter Principle," from the book by the same name authored by Peter and Raymond Hull.[9]

One of the biggest challenges of smart people in management or leadership positions is basic human nature. The human nature of these types of people is that they have a difficult time not answering questions. Others have turned to them frequently for answers because of their intelligence, so providing answers has become reflexive.

The Peter Principle references a study in which employees are promoted based on their success in previous jobs or prior projects until they reach a level where those skills no longer transition successfully. People like this haven't developed the soft skills to be able to lead in a way that will help others. While these employees were once recognized as both intelligent and talented, unless their skills continue to grow and improve, they will eventually max out what they can accomplish. Just because they're smart doesn't mean they can lead.[10]

My career began at the bottom of the food chain. When I graduated from college, I took a job selling copiers to businesses door-to-door, cold calling. I was given a couple of ZIP codes, a copier transporter, and access to demo copiers. Product and sales training lasted two weeks. Then, I was sent out to achieve a quota of four copier sales per month. This experience was the training ground for IBM, and my experience at IBM then prepared me for my job at US West. My experiences at US West prepared me for my job at Medtronic. As you can see, each role prepared me for the next. I learned what to do and what not to do from my leaders.

I always out-performed my peer group. Well, I *had to* significantly out-perform them to be considered for promotion. The fact that I had to do so much more to get promoted put me in a position to truly excel once the promotion took place. I was a lot different from other people who got promoted. Peers who were promoted ahead of me or into higher levels in the organization struggled. They weren't as prepared. I worked hard to refine my skills and capabilities to a point where I could be even more successful as I hit the ground running with each promotion. This has been a common theme throughout my career, and for all the extra effort, there has always been a reward.

When smart people don't succeed as leaders, it's often because higher-level leaders lost sight of a primary goal: to develop the capabilities of others to fulfill the mission and vision of the organization. A significant component of leading aligned organizations is how impactful time spent building other leaders can be. The more skills they develop, the more it helps the organization.

The Oracle of Information

The paradox of the smart person is that when their intelligence has been recognized long enough and loud enough, it's hard for them to admit when they no longer have the answers. What ends up happening is that they try to answer questions based on old knowledge or dated experiences. Due to the nature of the position, most leaders' thoughts and opinions are respected and deferred to. In many organizations, their answers become rules, regulations, or directives. Whether those answers are the best solutions or not is given little thought.

Once the smart person speaks, creativity gets diminished. For some, they'll go along with what has been said out of relief that they are not being asked to come up with a solution. Others will feel that same relief as well, but it's because they're lazy about their own creativity. However, others will remain quiet because the smartest person in the room spoke. Any other contribution will be viewed as "not so smart," and no one wants that to happen—especially in public.

Anything said after that could be construed as dissent. Moreover, empowerment is diminished when leaders act as the oracles of wisdom, which has a negative impact on accountability.

Seeking 360-Degree Feedback

Without gaining buy-in through input or discussion, the leader is fully accountable for the success or failure of his plan. These leaders miss out on opportunities to energize their organizations, foster critical thinking, and recognize people for what they do. Even if the teams and individuals do a decent job of executing a leader's plan, recognition for a "job well done" is not as well-received. It's like getting a trophy for participation. Yes, individuals showed up. Yes, they did their jobs, but they don't believe they were instrumental in the plan, rather mere puppets. There's limited excitement, motivation, or energy to carry over for the next project.

Consider the new leader returning to his or her post as a senior vice president after obtaining an MBA from Harvard. Imagine the first staff meeting when an employee asks a provocative question such as, "Will this strategy conflict with our culture?" The newly educated leader feels compelled to answer the question when, in reality, he or she should be using their "smarts" to gather input from the person asking the question and the group as a whole if this occurs in a team meeting. What they should be doing is asking questions in return, such as:

1. "What do you think about that?"
2. "Are there modifications that might benefit how the plan is adopted?"
3. "How might we better communicate the plan to bring clarity or get meaningful feedback?"

Not all leaders are comfortable asking for input. The problem isn't centered around domain knowledge; that is accepted. The issue is that not many leaders develop the skills to gain and benefit from 360-degree input. These include soft skills, emotional intelligence, and the ability to listen to and motivate others. Such skills are required for a domain expert to be successful in a leadership role.

In college, I competed in the decathlon. I was a good athlete. However, in my first year, I didn't know anything. I asked a lot of questions. The juniors and seniors helped me learn the ropes and provided me with the skills necessary to fill their leadership roles when the time came later in my collegiate experience.

The same thing happened at each of my jobs—I had to continue learning new leadership skills in order to be successful. I could lean on what I had built up, but that wasn't going to be enough for the new level of responsibility I was given. I had to humble myself to continuously seek out new knowledge and develop my skills.

Few direct reports or employees will speak up against a leader's opinions unless, and until, the leader creates an environment in which such feedback is not only acceptable, but welcome. This is how good leaders create opportunities to become great leaders—by opening up topics of discussion to the broader organization and taking advantage of the collective wisdom.

Questions Are the Answer

One of the most important skills to help the smart person is the art of listening. Smart people are used to having others ask them for advice and are usually more than happy to give it. However, the goal of leadership is to build a great team, not demonstrate superior knowledge. Drawing out the best in others is part of the job description of a leader. Instead of answering every question with a "best guess" based on experience, leaders who are willing to say, "I'm not really sure. What do you think?"—even if they *do* know the answer—encourage others to put their ideas on the table.

When employees present ideas and suggestions, strong leaders then dig deeper with additional questions: "Which of these ideas makes the most sense to you?" or "Which do you like best, and why?" This keeps the dialogue open and allows for great ideas to grow roots.

If those employees who are sharing ideas with leadership, either individually or in a team setting, get to a point where they hesitate, it falls on the leader to encourage them to think through their ideas a bit more, do some research, or engage with others on the topic. Each idea presented must be given its respective consideration. The next question then becomes, "Which one are you leaning toward as the best solution?" When one answer stands out as being the strongest, the dialogue might go like this:

"What is keeping you from executing it? Is it something I said or did?"

Most people will say, "No," not wanting to implicate the leader as someone who is blocking the path.

The next question is: "Then, let's talk about execution. What can I do to help you execute this plan that you have?"

They might say, "Could I get some time in a leadership meeting to explain what it is I am going to do to get buy-in from the other teams/leaders?"

It would then be up to the leader to create this opportunity. Conversations like these are how effective leaders get things moving and *keep* them moving—not by setting directives based solely on their limited knowledge and experience. The leader is relying on the "smarts" of others who may be closer to the issue at hand and have a deeper knowledge of the problems and potential solutions.

The benefit of this strategy is multifaceted.

1. A leader who defers to and values input from subordinates uplifts and empowers them to speak up. Typically, this circumstance charges the employee with increased energy for their role in the organization.

2. Those involved in generating ideas will be accountable for the success of those ideas. They will be more likely to put forth high-performance efforts in implementing their ideas, as they will feel responsible for the outcome. They own it.

3. When individuals or teams accomplish the work they helped to design and are recognized for it, they will know the recognition is sincere. They are not being recognized for completing tasks related to someone else's ideas or plans. Such recognition creates a reverberating effect throughout the organization. After all, how many times have we seen someone get recognized, and the applause reflected an underwhelming golf clap? This is a common occurrence in command-and-control cultures where leaders are viewed as the smartest people on the team. When leaders recognize employees who follow mandates, that recognition falls flat.

4. Other individuals and teams see that the organization is willing to take calculated risks. Strong leaders are open, value input, and are willing to get behind good ideas no matter where they come from. This drives real empowerment, creating a higher level of energy across the entire organization.

Hiring smart people is vital to every organization—the greater the talent, the greater the impact. However, when those smart people move into leadership positions, guidance must be provided as to how to use their expertise in fulfillment of the mission and vision through the development of leadership skills.

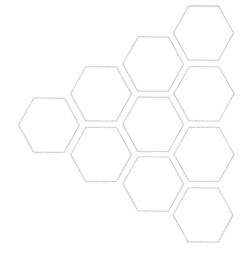

CHAPTER 16

THE ALIGNMENT
PLAYBOOK

J ust as coaches develop playbooks of tactics and methods
for creating winning teams, leaders must develop "plays"
necessary to bring the various individuals within the organization into alignment. Organizational success is often linked to
having an inspiring vision, a clear mission, and strong values.
But without employee buy-in, these concepts are worthless.
While employee *engagement* is essential to an organization's
success, alignment is arguably even more important.

As an example, consider a 400-meter relay race. The winning
team carries the baton past the finish line first. The strategy
is the same for all the teams. The direction toward the finish
line is like the alignment that exists between employees and
an organization's vision and goals. The *speed* of each runner is

akin to engagement. To win, every runner in the team must run fast (i.e., be engaged with the organization) but also remain in the same lane as other team members with a keen eye toward the finish line. However, the implementation of the strategy might be very different. This is where an alignment playbook becomes essential.

Lining Up the Crosshairs

Alignment within teams begins with aligning the organization's leaders. When we talk about alignment, think about it in terms of crosshairs in a rifle scope. There is the latitudinal crosshair, which is left to right. This is where it is determined if the leadership team across divisions or departments is fully on board with the strategy of the organization. Latitudinal alignment involves looking fellow leaders in the eyes and asking:

1. Are we on the same page with the **mission**—where we want to go? This question is not meant to be accusatory or inflammatory, but investigative. As described in the topic of communication, there might be a mismatch of frequencies. Various leaders may have interpreted information in different ways. Having humility and curiosity about why there are gaps in understanding or agreement should lead to stronger alignment.
2. Are we in agreement with the **philosophies** and **methods** that will be used to connect the rest of the organization to our mission and vision? Having discussions around disparity might uncover inconsistencies in messaging.
3. Are we on the same page about the **processes** we're going to use to lead and communicate throughout the journey?

Perhaps aspects of the plan aren't clear, or other ways to accomplish the goal will be revealed.

When leaders across teams are in agreement and purposefully aligned with the mission, vision, and strategic plan of the organization, then, and only then, should they move on to the longitudinal work of implementation. Longitudinal crosshairs run from top to bottom in a scope. This involves the key elements necessary to drive alignment down through the organization department by department, team by team to the individual employees. What follows are the key points that need to be addressed initially.

- Point A: Making it clear what the world will look like if we accomplish the mission.
- Point B: Sharing the broader mission in a manner that evokes coherence and can easily be remembered, recited, and referred to when decisions need to be made.
- Point C: Ensuring that it's clear at the individual contributor level how their role impacts the mission.

Those are the high-level points that are part of the leader's alignment playbook. If they are not clear, there will be a lack of alignment or commitment.

Key Performance Indicators

Leaders use measurement tools such as key performance indicators (KPIs) to gain insight into the progress of strategic plans. These are quantifiable measures related to how well objectives are being met. KPIs provide the roadmap for fulfilling the mission. They are the mile markers along the journey that break down the mission and its strategic plan into bite-sized pieces and reflect the metrics that support it. KPIs show all stakeholders how the success of the plan is being evaluated every step of the way.

In Gino Wickman's book, *Traction*,[11] he says, "Successful businesses operate with a crystal-clear vision that is shared by everyone. They have the right people in the right seats. They have a pulse on their operations by watching and managing a handful of numbers on a weekly basis. They identify and solve issues promptly in an open and honest environment. They *document their processes* and ensure that they are followed by everyone. They *establish priorities* for each employee and ensure that a high level of trust, communication, and accountability exists on each team." This is an excellent basis for the development of any leader's alignment playbook. Having data-driven insights into the level of alignment in an organization and where it exists—or doesn't—is crucial. Think about how much more effective a leader can be when there's information pointing to exactly where there are issues or weaknesses.

If there are behaviors within the organization that aren't consistent with the plan, leaders need to go to the source to determine what needs to be done, whether it's a change in communication or a change in the plan. It's critical for leaders to see the broader organization and know where potential breakdowns, especially in communication, occur, and work to prevent them. This is where the leadership skills of troubleshooting and problem solving—through questions—become most valuable to the organization. Here are just a few critical questions to ask:

1. How did we get here? What was the cause? When the stopping point or blockage is discovered, it's time for a 360-degree analysis of what contributed to it. It's rarely one single thing or individual that causes a breakdown in the flow of the strategic plan, and it will likewise rarely require a single solution.

2. How do we get from here to where we need to be? This question should be repeatedly asked throughout the implementation of a strategic plan because new knowledge and information is being produced throughout the process. This information may warrant adjustments to how the next moves are made.

3. What tools or resources are needed? Has it been revealed that different tools are required to get to the next benchmark than expected? Are more resources needed, or do they need to be distributed differently? Is additional training required? This resource question is often where barriers present themselves. Competing objectives or interests are the main issues that come up. Even in aligned organizations, there can and will be conflicts when it comes to allocating resources. With a finite amount of resources available, choices are made and may need to be made again differently. This is where aligned latitudinal leadership across teams is very important. Latitudinal conversations at each level can help realign resources and timing toward agreed-upon projects and initiatives. This will help alleviate silos across teams, foster collaboration, and bring forward best practices.

This process is not rocket science. However, it takes a high level of commitment to gain the most benefit from it. By establishing

KPIs, the leadership team is able to measure success and to track whether or not everyone is performing the right tasks at the best level to get the organization to its destination. What gets measured gets done. KPIs provide a checkpoint for leaders to assess the trajectory toward the goal. They help leaders to determine if the target will be hit given the current course, speed, altitude, weather conditions, and so on. With the data KPIs provide, course corrections can be made as necessary to achieve success. At the end of the day, it's the implementation of the plan along the longitudinal line that gets the organization to its target.

Adjusting the Course and Processes

Once crosshairs are lined up and KPIs have been established to measure performance to plan, things will, inevitably, go differently than expected. It's impossible for every step and contingency to be mapped out and addressed. This is a great place to lean on alignment principles to make course adjustments to stay aligned with the mission and plan.

When challenges do arise, everyone can look to the mission and the plan for solutions. If the answers can't be easily identified, a detour or workaround might be needed. Or, it may be that another look through the crosshairs is called for. Did we have improper assumptions? Is the challenge due to a disconnect between leaders (latitudinal) or because of a communication breakdown down the organizational chart (longitudinal)? Or is it related to the systems and processes being used?

If there is a disconnect between any of the activities and the mission, it should become obvious where the challenge originated and simple to help those involved find a resolution. The mission and vision are the compasses by which all decisions and actions are measured.

The most common disconnect is a simple misunderstanding due to incomplete knowledge. With incomplete knowledge, individuals may hesitate to perform or misperform, causing a bottleneck in workflow. As an example, let's say you believe you have broken a bone. During your visit to the doctor, she begins examining you by taking your temperature. You may not understand why, and thus begin to doubt the doctor's qualifications—you may even think about finding another doctor. The doctor's actions or instructions seem irrelevant to your situation. When the doctor communicates that it's common for the body temperature to rise after breaking a bone, your understanding increases and you stop resisting. You now understand that it's all going according to protocol. This is not to say that individuals on your team lack knowledge in general; they may just not have a complete enough understanding of all the aspects of the plan that affect them in their roles.

When leaders appreciate the value of an alignment playbook, they create a point of reference for themselves and others when challenges arise. That common resource that shows the alignment between mission and vision, systems and processes, and objectives helps determine the best actions to take to achieve the goal.

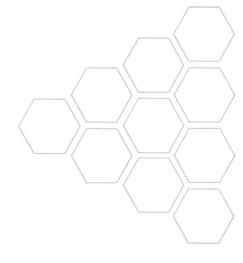

CHAPTER 17

TEAM ALIGNMENT

G etting individuals aligned with purpose to the mission and vision is important to the success of any organization. Thus, leaders must invest the time to get their direct reports aligned. Otherwise, strategic plans lose their clarity as they are communicated down the ranks. School districts, in particular, struggle with this. The life expectancy of a school superintendent is two-and-a-half years. The tenure of a superintendent's "cabinet" is much longer. It can be tough for leaders to get the cabinet aligned knowing they will have a new boss shortly.

As previously mentioned, leaders must be aligned latitudinally. Each division, department, or team leader must then promote alignment longitudinally. This is where leaders get down in the trenches and use their skills to create alignment within teams.

No two players on a team will have the exact same skillsets. It follows then that they will not play the same roles or have the same responsibilities. The strategy for developing solid teams is to search for employees who have complementary strengths and skills. The job of the leadership then becomes one of:

1. Identifying the skills necessary to get the job done.
2. Putting people in positions where they can contribute and succeed.
3. Creating a synergistic culture that defines, rewards, and promotes success.

It may behoove leaders, whether new to an organization or new to a leadership position, to evaluate each member of the team as to their strengths and the roles they play. This is where many organizations use the S.W.O.T. analysis. This analysis was developed in the 1960s by Albert Humphrey, who led a research project at Stanford University on why corporate planning failed. The letters in S.W.O.T. stand for: Strengths, Weaknesses, Opportunities, and Threats. The value of a S.W.O.T. analysis is that it generates a lot of information in a way that's easy to understand. That information can be a foundation upon which to draw a real-world picture of what the team has and what's missing. It also alludes to the things that cannot be controlled or influenced, which is of tremendous help when placing employees in roles and prioritizing activities. Having the best people in the right roles goes a long way toward establishing team alignment.

While determining skills and assigning roles, it's also critical to identify that your team players are willing to do the work that is required. When the organization's mission and vision are aligned with their purpose, people will gladly do the work to fulfill the strategic plan. They, in effect, tell leaders and their teammates that they can be counted on. When everyone knows they can rely on each other, trust is attained, and organizations move at the speed of trust.

Dirty Work

In creating alignment within teams and organizations, there will inevitably be some dirty work required. This may involve making decisions about closing a department down, moving people to new positions, or changing job descriptions. It may even involve terminating someone's employment. There are countless things that leaders must do to drive alignment. During these times, they can find themselves on the receiving end of anger, disappointment, and mistrust. Once those tasks are completed, the leader's job then involves rebuilding teams and creating re-alignment. At times, that requires maniacal focus (and some good Scotch) as the leader may feel as though they've "taken one for the team."

Karl Malone played in the NBA from 1985 to 2004, in the position of power forward. He earned the nickname of "The Mailman" because he always "delivered." At 6'9" and 256 pounds, he was a force to be reckoned with. Those who played defense against him had to be prepared to take charge. That meant standing in his way and letting him run you over, knowing that it was necessary to stop him if your team was to beat his. Those defenders knew there was a chance they'd be knocked down, possibly even sitting out for the rest of the game. Yet, they chose to do the job that was necessary. They put their own strengths into play for the organization. They sacrificed their health for the common goal of winning.

Sacrificing health is never expected in a corporate structure. However, not every job is glamorous. Yet, every position contributes. Remember the story of JFK and the janitor?

Even those who handle the dirty work, whether they're leaders or employees, need to have their contributions recognized. Recognize them and their value to the organization as a whole. Once the dirty work is done, give those players opportunities to succeed in other ways. No one wants to be the "bad guy" all the time—even if they're good at it. Even Dirty Harry had friends!

Maximizing Team Alignment

There are many similarities between sports teams and company teams when it comes to strategy and the importance of alignment. Let's look at the particular set of strategies used by relay teams. First, each runner must commit to the mission of the team. They each must set a goal of performing at their highest levels. Then, they need to acknowledge the strengths and weaknesses of each runner. This can be tough, as no one wants to admit they may be the weakest link. However, what's more important is how the team can work together to maximize the strength of each member of the group.

It's the responsibility of each relay runner to establish a solid time in their portion of the race to put those following in good position. The runners also need to practice how the handoffs will go before the race. There is a specific placement of the hand. There is a communication that takes place that lets the receiver know how to extend their hand. The baton is extended to the right spot at the right time so the next runner can take it in stride, which will catapult them to run faster during their portion of the race.

At the 2008 Summer Olympics, the Japanese men's relay team won the silver medal. It was the first time their 4 X 100m men's relay team had won a medal. Even though they did not have the fastest individual runners, their strategy and precision in passing the baton made the difference between getting a medal and not placing at all. They understood the impact the handoff made on the overall race. They practiced it daily. The placement of the four runners was evaluated, tested, measured, and adjusted by their coach. Their handoffs of the baton were meticulous. By concentrating their individual performance efforts on the end result of a team win, their leaders were able to get them to achieve together what none of them could have accomplished individually.

Organizations do not always have to have the best talent to succeed. In fact, having the best talent can be a distraction. When there is a clear "best" player, if they're not team-focused, their presence can create distractions, jealousy, and infighting. Or there can be a reliance on the "star," leading to synergy loss. When you have players who can focus on the end goal and align their talents for the greater good, the idea of having superstars falls by the wayside. When all are moving in the same direction with a common goal, greater success can be had.

Handling Promotions

When the time comes for someone on the team to be promoted, the focus cannot be limited to the opportunities in their new position. There needs to be a 360-degree evaluation of how such a change will impact the team. Who's moving up? Who will take their place? What are the strengths and weaknesses of each? How much crossover training is required, and for how long? It's in the best interest of the organization to keep previous positions filled with the right players when someone gets promoted.

When leaders are moving up within the organization, they will want their legacy to manifest. Creating precision alignment before a handoff to an incoming leader (or employee) is vital to the continued success of the team. The smoother the transition, the greater the opportunity to continue the work that is being done and accomplish the next set of goals for the team or division.

This is, in effect, succession planning. A team member moves on, and another one steps up. Having a plan for reducing "organ rejection" and promoting adoption is critical. Onboarding and training are necessary, as well. However, establishing a common goal and fostering accountability is what drives alignment, and ultimately, excellence.

CHAPTER 18

THE LEADERSHIP
PLAYBOOK

"Leadership is not about being in charge,
it is about taking care of people in your charge."
– Simon Sinek

M anagement literature is replete with leadership theories, models, and styles. At the practice level, however, leadership is all about getting people to leverage their skills for the common good of all stakeholders. This includes those within the organization and those in the broader community.

A masterful example of involving the broader community in the success of an organization is Amazon. When the leadership at Amazon begins the process of opening warehouses in new communities, everyone gets on board. Community leaders understand the value of having an employer with such a great reputation come into the area. Real estate is purchased, which positively impacts the tax base. Jobs are created. Workers need places to live and services close by. The entire community can benefit.

On the inside of organizations, it is only when every employee sees the vision as personally desirable and ascribes to the strategies and tactics to get there that organizations will see accelerated improvements in performance. This is what leads to the achievement of desired business outcomes.

It's up to the leaders to help employees see the vision clearly. There is no single tactic for making this happen. Leaders need to develop their skills to include a variety of ways to communicate, encourage teamwork, and drive accountability—which are all part of the alignment puzzle.

Creating organizational alignment is a critical responsibility for an organization's leaders. Indeed, those same leaders who define their organization's visions are responsible for creating the roadmaps to get there and make calculated course corrections along the way. The attainment of alignment is dependent on the leader's ability to inspire his or her followers to pursue a common mission with energy and zeal.

Leadership is not a title—it's a role. Just because someone reaches the leadership level in the organizational chart doesn't necessarily mean they are effective leaders. They are given leadership responsibility and, hopefully, will fulfill the role well. In this role, they may need to act as inspirational messengers or full-time caretakers. It is the responsibility of the leader to develop the skills required to fulfill whichever strategy is called for at any given time. Those skills will be applied to whatever "play" is necessary to deliver messages, ask the right questions, think through solutions, develop strategic plans, and "sell" those plans throughout the organization. The role of leadership is not static; it's dynamic. Skills that prove effective with leadership peers might be different from skills that need to be used when communicating with or developing direct reports.

Leaders set the direction of the organization. They communicate that direction verbally, as well as through their actions. As appropriate, leaders may designate others to lead the charge, so to speak, on a project or initiative. As business advisor Dan Sullivan says, "In every organization, there are 'human benchmarks'—certain individuals whose behavior becomes a model for everyone else—shining examples that others admire and emulate." When these "human benchmarks" are designated, the leaders' role becomes one of allocating resources, as well as monitoring progress and results. This selfless act of leadership, stepping away from the limelight, speaks to leading from behind. Glory is trumpeted by accomplishment, not by position.

Organizational Alignment is Not Accidental

Faulty business strategies or poor implementation are often identified as the root cause of a business failing to achieve its goals. But it's really the people behind those strategies and their implementation that make or break the strategy. Organizational alignment is not accidental. Creating it requires open, multi-directional communication. It needs leaders to set clear and ethical goals for themselves and others. It requires leaders to give honest and timely feedback with the objective of enabling individuals to increase their own performance levels, not just to criticize or lay blame when plans fail.

Effective leaders are able to combine diverse views and ideas and coherently synthesize them into what's best for the organization. More importantly, they are able to inspire even those whose ideas are not adopted to see why the chosen option is better and commit to that path. Organizational interests must come before individual interests.

Organizations need strong leaders to create and sustain alignment because not every member buys into (or remains bought into) the organization's vision and strategy at all times. New employees need to understand the mission and the role they play in accomplishing it. This can be achieved through effective training, or better yet, effective *screening*. Finding individuals who align around the mission prior to hiring means they require less training, are more productive, and less likely to quit.

At regular intervals, effective leaders must gauge the degree to which there is alignment within their organizations and take actions to optimize it further as necessary. This may require leaders to:

- Paint a picture of a more desirable future (the vision). A perfect example of this is the "I Have a Dream" speech by Dr. Martin Luther King Jr.
- Get people charged up and convinced that this future is worth the effort (buy-in). This is accomplished by sharing the stories of the consumers of the organization's products and services.

When the fact that the employees' efforts make a difference in the lives of others is shared, those employees tend to further align their purpose with the organization's mission and vision.

- Create an environment of accountability focused on outcome, not effort. From the book, *Traction*, "What gets measured gets done."[12]

Strong leaders are consistently proactive when it comes to organizational alignment. With alignment, innovation thrives, and superior results are delivered to all stakeholders.

Stand, Float, or Charge?

There are many different forms of leadership, and it is up to the leader to determine which form is most effective at any given moment. The strategies implemented by leadership will be different when announcing growth and the launch of new products or services than when announcing change due to failure to acquire increased market share. Let's say an external or internal event shakes the team's faith in the leader, or the strategy being executed. It falls to the leaders to determine how to address those situations. Regaining the trust of employees may require openness and a dose of humility.

Even when no major event occurs to interrupt the plan, leaders must recognize when even long-term, dedicated employees need to be rejuvenated, and possibly reinvigorated, with the vision. Leaders are prepared to invest time and effort in realigning employees with the vision, especially when strategic plans require a lengthy time frame to implement.

The culture of an organization is driven by employees but *steered* by leadership in top-down leadership organizations. A command-and-control leader typically looks for other command-and control leaders to hire within the organization's structure. The strength of harmony between structure and culture is a critical component of alignment. Some organizations have a culture in which it is unacceptable to push back against plans and to challenge certain types of leaders. Depending upon the type of organization, this could stifle attempts at alignment.

In such organizations, employees feel they must simply accept leadership direction without question. In a paramilitary organization, there is little or no room or tolerance for pushback against leadership. Lives are at stake, and every directive is part of a greater strategy. Lives can be put in danger if people down the line of command receive ambiguous messages, leaving them to interpret for themselves. Or, if they "get creative" and deviate from the directive, the results can be perilous.

While creativity wouldn't be considered a pillar that would score high in such organizations, communication and accountability should. In many law enforcement agencies, however, we've seen that communication scores are surprisingly low. In many cases, this is because, even though law enforcement communicates regularly, they may not have regular conversations about connecting behaviors and actions with mission and vision, which our question specifically asks. Also, in some instances, consistently holding themselves and others accountable to acting per the stated, written mission has also lagged. The result has sometimes meant the growth of an "unwritten mission and culture" within such organizations that has created a large gap between what citizens need and what is being provided.

As seen with the killing of George Floyd in May 2020, as well as the killing of other Black Americans by police, the stated mission of some agencies—which, in general, has been "To Protect and Serve our Community"—has been overrun by this "unwritten" culture. The sad result is that these agencies which have neglected their accountability have applied different rules and practices toward Black and other communities of color. This dynamic reflects the lack of alignment of our American culture and history with our mission, as stated in the Declaration of Independence that, "We hold these truths to be self-evident, that all men are created equal, that they are endowed by their Creator with certain unalienable Rights, that among these are Life, Liberty and the pursuit of Happiness."

In contrast, bottom-up organizations project the leaders as a hologram, reflecting their collective interests. An example of this is the Electoral College. The Electoral College, every four years through its constitutionally mandated electors, elects the president and vice president of the United States based on the voting totals of each state and the District of Columbia. It's the same with the leader who is part of a bottom-up organization. The thought process among individuals is this: "We've taken the time to define who we are, what we're all about, what we espouse, and what we value, and we've all signed off on it." Leaders are put in place to reflect the values of the organization. This is more likely to occur with organizations where the leadership is appointed or elected: politics, associations, or school boards.

In some company cultures, aggressive leadership is accepted as the norm. The quickest way to determine if an organization has aggressive leadership is when internal surveys are deployed, and there is low participation. Individuals don't want to say the wrong thing for fear of reprisal. Or, they just don't believe anything will come from responding. Another way to identify aggressive leadership is that there are very few questions asked after a leader has spoken. The interpretation by the listeners is that the words spoken were *directives.*

In other organizations, aggressive leadership would be detrimental. An aggressive leader might stand on top of a hill with a bullhorn, shouting orders to get things done. His messages are viewed as directives and are often too broad and generic. The followers might not understand which "hill" the leader is referencing. Other examples of this type of directives are:

"Increase revenue by 8%!"

"Launch 30 new products this year!"

Those might be the goals, but there must be a strategy or structure developed to accomplish them.

Another type of leader may float on top of the hill, observing rather than directing. Some of these leaders are hands-off and passive because they don't understand what's going on. They view their roles as to be seen as a figurehead with little to no interaction. This type of leader can be seen in well-aligned organizations. When leaders have done their work of alignment well, the organization runs like a well-oiled machine, and there is little need for the leader to be in the trenches, but rather to allow the work to flow and remain accessible.

Still other leaders may charge up the hill themselves, shouting for the others to follow. Leaders cannot expect employees to follow them anywhere without a clear goal and strategy in place. The only time employees will follow leaders without having a clear goal is when the leader has a track record of success and the full trust of the employee base. In this case, the employees' faith in this leader is strong. They're thinking, "This individual pulled us out of a tough spot before. We trust that they can help us resolve this situation, as well."

Leaders who develop a wide range of strategies will achieve the greatest success. Being able to flex with each situation rather than relying on a single style of leadership will allow leaders to encourage growth and innovation through collective knowledge and efforts. This leads to trust and speeds up the achievement of the mission and vision of the organization.

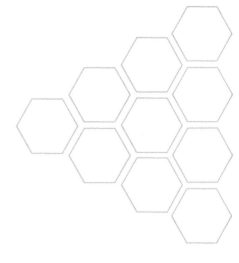

CHAPTER 19

THE ALIGNMENT GAP

The alignment gap is the space that exists between where an organization is and where it wants to be to achieve its mission and vision. All organizations have gaps. This is not to say that people are slacking. In fact, everyone may be working very hard. They may be seeking ways to improve productivity, and be committed to goals, yet still not be in alignment with the mission and vision. Determining where and how large the gaps are requires an evaluation or assessment. The results of the assessment will point to the biggest gaps in alignment so plans can be developed to start closing them.

Our research indicates that average organizations demonstrate around 76 percent alignment in their leadership teams—1st and 2nd level leadership. This means there is approximately 24 percent *mis*alignment, as noted in the graphic. This could mean that one out of four leaders is misaligned, or that all leaders are misaligned within some of the pillars—or any combination of these situations. While 24 percent misalignment may not sound like a huge number, what's important to realize is that the degree of misalignment increases the deeper you go into an organization, which is seen by the other two bars in the graphic. No level can be more aligned than the level above it simply because leaders can only effectively communicate what they understand, believe in, and are committed to.

% Aligned Responses

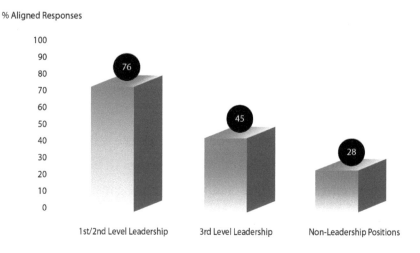

Compare this to a compass heading. If the goal is to sail from Hawaii to Los Angeles and the course heading is off by 10 feet for every hundred feet traveled, that would be 10 percent, or less than half the misalignment noted above. That doesn't seem like much, especially when you leave port in Hawaii. However, the greater the distance you travel at that heading, the farther you move away from your intended destination. For the roughly 2,500-mile journey, you would reach land about

250 miles away from your destination. That would mean you would end up around Monterey, California. That's a beautiful location, but you wanted to be in LA.

Now, imagine being 24 percent off course! You might end up at the California/Oregon state line—which is also a beautiful place, but not where you want to be. Every bit of misalignment takes the organization farther away from achieving its mission. We'll get into the impact of this misalignment when we look at third level leadership shortly.

Assessing Where You Are

Scores of assessment tools have been developed and implemented over the years. Many organizations have used engagement surveys to determine the sentiments of employees in hopes of figuring out ways to improve performance. However, those assessments do not measure engagement against any of the vital pillars of alignment. It's one thing to be engaged in a role, but if what is being done is not contributing to the mission and vision of the organization, the output may be counterproductive—reducing performance rather than enhancing it.

If you will, remember the Greek king, Sisyphus. He was tasked with pushing a huge boulder up a steep hill only to have it roll back down as he neared the top. His only focus was on the present challenge, never considering the purpose of his task. It's the same with many employees who punch a time clock. They just put their heads down and do their work without considering its broader purpose. Without a clear purpose to their work, burnout is imminent. Aligned employees are less apt to burn out because of the element of purpose. They know why they're doing what they're doing and achieve self-actualization by doing it. The key to fixing gaps in alignment that don't take purpose into consideration is an alignment assessment.

This type of assessment measures the effectiveness of each leader or individual within the nine pillars of alignment covered in this book. It points to how unintentional and inconsistent communication creates roadblocks and reveals the level and degree of accountability each leader has and how empowered they feel in their positions on the organizational chart. An alignment assessment also helps organizations discover silos that interfere with teamwork and whether or not the organization has a culture that encourages creativity.

The purpose of an alignment assessment is to establish a baseline as to how deeply each leader has bought into the overall mission and vision and how effective they are at communicating the organization's messages. Once alignment gaps are identified, action plans can be developed to help leaders practice ways to drive greater alignment across divisions and down through the ranks. This requires some work.

The value in performing this type of assessment is that it will generate a visual for the organization, and the results can be depicted numerically. The higher the number, the more aligned the organization is. This can be likened to an IQ test. The data from the assessment identifies the extent of misalignment, finds which areas have misalignments, and indicates where more effort should be made and what best practices may need to be developed.

Alignment at one level cannot be higher than the level(s) above it. In misaligned or semi-aligned organizations, there are typically significant gaps between the second and third levels of leadership. The first two levels of leadership are generally in agreement on mission, vision, and strategic plans, well, at least to a 76% level. However, even when the second-level leaders are involved in developing core strategies and plans, those leaders may not do a great job of cascading the proper messages to the next level and garnering alignment commitments from their direct reports.

The enlargement of the alignment gap between the second and third levels has been proven similar across various types of organizations: corporate, education, and law enforcement. Our analysis (seen in the above chart) shows a 30% drop in alignment between these two levels! Leaders at the second level are quality people. However, they fail at guiding third level leaders in transferring the mission, vision, and strategic plan into actionable practice that will cascade throughout the organization. Once these gaps are identified, however, the first and second level leaders can develop strategies to strengthen the messages related to mission and vision that are delivered down through the various levels within the organization. Using aligned leadership practices and techniques as outlined throughout this book will go a long way toward shrinking gaps between levels.

Purpose Bridges the Gap

The key to increasing results through alignment is purpose. When we add purpose to our work, the risk of burnout decreases. This means establishing purpose both in the leadership and within the teams and individuals throughout the organization. When people work with purpose, there is lower turnover, fewer sick days are taken, and performance at peak levels increases.

If what you love to do is give money away to those in need, and you have an unlimited source of that money, you would never get tired of doing the job. The opposite would happen. You would be so motivated and satisfied with giving money away that you would gladly do it 24/7/365. That's what happens when you add the element of purpose to your work and help others discover their purpose as well. This involves a realization that there is something bigger than one person's contribution to the goal of the larger organization. Because people want to be involved in something that makes a difference, they will lean in. Their focus will increase, they won't tire as easily, and will be less apt to show up late. They will be fully entrenched in getting the job done right at the right time. This sentiment has been expressed through the centuries by those considered quite wise.

- "The purpose of life is not to be happy. It is to be useful, to be honorable, to be compassionate, to have it make some difference that you have lived and lived well." – Ralph Waldo Emerson
- "The mystery of human existence lies not in just staying alive, but in finding something to live for." – Fyodor Dostoyevsky
- "True happiness... is not attained through self-gratification, but through fidelity to a worthy purpose." – Helen Keller

According to a May 2019 article in Newsweek magazine: "People who have a sense of purpose in life appear to live longer, according to the latest research linking this outlook to a person's quality of life and to better physical and mental health."[13]

The authors of the study published in the journal *JAMA Network Open* looked at data collected from 6,985 adults who were signed up to the Health and Retirement Study on people ages 50 and above in the U.S. The team looked at a group who completed a questionnaire in 2006 about their purpose in life and used it to come up with a score. On average, the participants were 68.6 years old. Next, the scientists looked at causes of death in the group between 2006 and 2010 with variables including their demographic, marital status, race, and education level. Lifestyle choices like smoking and drinking were also noted.

Purpose was defined by the authors as a self-organizing life aim that stimulates goals, promotes healthy behaviors, and gives meaning to life.

The data revealed that the more the participants felt they had a purpose in life, the lower their risk of dying. This result remained even when the scientists adjusted their calculations for factors that could affect their scores, such as a participants' sociodemographic status and their health.

To fully imbue purpose in the day-to-day activities of employees, Medtronic did something very interesting. The company would bring in a group of patients who had received Medtronic devices to thank them for their business. It was a way to get the patients to share their stories, creating an atmosphere where the engineers who were developing and building these devices were able to see the outcome of their work. Therefore, their sense of purpose for their work was invigorated.

Imagine meeting Grandpa, who is now 80 years old and has a pacemaker and more energy than he's had in 10 years, telling of time spent with his grandchildren and the joy that has brought to the lives of the entire family. It was impossible to leave that room without having had an emotional reaction about how each person's work impacted the lives of those we served.

To further assist my team members in discovering and enhancing their purpose within Medtronic, I relied on the Medtronic mission and vision, which is to alleviate pain, restore health, and extend life.

I would ask the following questions:

"Do you know that the device you are selling is the best in the market?"

"Do you know as you gain market share you are extending the lives of people who would not have that benefit if it were not for the work that you are doing?"

"Do you know why this community is beholden to you? It is not because of how much money you make. Rather, it is because of the work that you do that alleviates pain, restores health, and extends life, and ultimately everybody benefits from that. On a daily basis, as you go about gaining market share, you are living the vision and mission of our company, and the world benefits from that. I am here to say to you thank you. Let us not lose sight of living the mission and vision."

When leaders approach others as personable human beings rather than driven and driving taskmasters, their messages are better received. The message is that, "Your work is fulfilling the mission, has broad implications, and speaks to our purpose!" Strong leaders in every organization work hard to find gaps in alignment, then to close those gaps. Find the purpose of your work and bring it to life. Tell the stories. Help people find their purposes as they relate to the mission and vision of the organization. Different strategies are required depending on where the gaps are and how large, but once discovered and dealt with, organizations become much more aligned, thus resulting in higher performance.

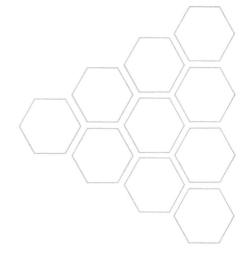

CHAPTER 20

ALIGNMENT QUESTIONS

"We thought that we had the answers,
it was the questions we had wrong."
– Bono

I t is only when you are effective at asking the right questions that you can get to the right solutions. It doesn't matter if the questions are related to the performance of individuals, teams, and divisions or to the overall company mission, strategy, structure, and culture. If you're not asking the right questions, you will never get the answers you need to devise the right solutions. This may result in double-loop learning, which happens when the first "loop" or answer to a problem needs to be modified because experience proves that the first loop didn't provide a satisfactory solution.

An example of double-loop learning happened when the airport commission at a large Midwest airport was charged with finding a solution to a specific customer complaint. The complaint was about having too long a wait for bags in the baggage claim area. The airport commission went to work to determine how to increase the speed of moving the bags from the planes to the baggage area. After some consideration, it was decided that an upgrade in their delivery system was needed. The commission spent $3.5 million on new conveyor belts and systems to speed up the process. With these changes, they were successful in reducing the time it took to deliver bags to baggage claim by 40 percent.

While 40 percent seems like a substantial improvement, the result was a minimal decrease in complaints because the flyers were still getting to baggage claim ahead of their bags and having to wait. Upon further investigation of the complaints, what people wanted was to get to baggage claim at the same time as their bags. This caused the commission to consider a different solution. Further analysis determined that the moving walkways were transporting people so fast that they were able to get to baggage claim incredibly quickly. The second "loop" determination was to reduce the speed of the moving walkways going toward baggage claim. Making this change only cost $10,000. The real question was not, "How do we get bags into the baggage claim area faster?" It was, "How do we close the gap between the time people and their baggage arrive in the baggage claim area?" If different questions had been asked before money was spent, the second answer would have resolved the complaints much more economically.

As stated earlier in the book, leaders must be good at asking questions *and* listening to the answers. The big difference in leadership and the results garnered is in the quality of the questions being asked. When leaders do not get the answers they're seeking it's wise to reconsider the questions being asked. The entire alignment assessment practice was founded on the realization that when it came to improving performance to the highest levels, the wrong questions were being asked.

Questions for Leaders

When considering the alignment of your organization, there are three key questions to ask those in leadership positions—including yourself. The answers to these three questions will form the baseline for how to proceed toward a higher level of alignment that will move everyone closer to peak performance and the fulfillment of the mission.

Question #1: Is organizational alignment important to you?
Chances are that the answer to that question will be "yes." Everyone you ask, even if they don't fully understand what "alignment" means, will assume it's of value. So, you will get agreement with the concept of alignment.

John Kelley was my boss at US West. He reported directly to the CEO. I will never forget his ability to take very complex things and simplify them.

After our initial alignment measurement at Medtronic, I could clearly see that there was misalignment, even among the leadership team. So, I engaged John to provide a different, external voice and walk us down the path of what it would look like to be aligned at the leadership level—from a latitudinal perspective.

To do this, John came in and provided that roadmap. He grabbed the financial statements and delved into the shareholder meeting notes. He laid out the direction the organization was going in a surgical manner. Based on his study of the financials, he was able to quickly rank the priorities of the organization. He was then able to look at my region and break down how we, specifically, contributed in each and every one of those priorities and explain it clearly.

He also spoke with each of my direct reports and described specifically how their roles contributed to the overall mission and vision. He explained how they had to work cross-functionally in a manner that exuded synergy to propel the region to optimal performance. When we came out of that session, not only were people clear on what they needed to do in terms of working as a team, but also how to provide the appropriate, consistent messaging to others. The bottom line was that the leaders in my region gained a clearer understanding of alignment, so when they agreed it was important, it was with clarity and enthusiasm.

Question #2: How do you measure alignment today?

Research shows that few in leadership positions truly understand how to measure alignment. Leaders are often conflicted by this question. Answers range from "We do an annual engagement study" to "We use internal surveys to assess climate." Human resources professionals struggle in this space as well because they are charged with supporting leadership and don't want to make waves that could lead to career displacement. So, human resource leads push archaic tools of measurement that do not correlate with performance, such as employee satisfaction surveys, climate studies, and engagement surveys. Most feedback to this question is related to whether or not quotas are being met, the level of employee job satisfaction, and the results of engagement studies.

> I once went to HealthPartners, a health maintenance organization in Minnesota, and met with key leaders in human resources. I asked two questions, the answers to which would be very telling. The first question was, "How long have you been measuring engagement?" The answer was "20 years." The second question was, "Have you been able to correlate your engagement scores with business outcomes?" The answer was, "Absolutely not." This answer led me to ask a third question, "So, why do you continue to measure engagement?" The answer was, "Because executive compensation is tied to it." This sort of flawed logic is common in many organizations. It needs to be understood that there are ways of measuring things that matter when the goal is deriving the outcomes that are sought. That's more valuable to the organization than leaders slapping themselves on the back and awarding themselves bonuses for employees reporting that they're engaged.

Question #3: Is it possible to be *engaged* and not *aligned*? This is the ultimate question. It's truly an a-ha moment for many leaders when they grasp the difference between engagement and alignment and realize they are not measuring alignment at all. When we think about an *engaged* workforce, this is a group of people that are working very hard. While hard work is of great value to an organization, if it is not aligned to the strategic plan and committed to with purpose, the end result will not be as impactful as it could be.

I learned the importance of asking the right questions from my father. He would often consider the results of my lawn mowing efforts at age 15 and ask, "Son, is this your best work?" The question was often somewhat rhetorical as the answer was obvious—it wasn't. To get me to improve my level of performance, his next question was, "When will we see your best work?" What he was doing was calibrating expectations with outcome. While I had been engaged in doing the yardwork, my actions were not initially aligned with his expectations. Once I realized the difference, the result was that I rose to his expectations and delivered a perfectly manicured lawn.

That simple line of questioning became a driving force for me to always ask what else could be done. How could I do something different—how could I do it better? How could my team perform at a higher level? How could we, as an organization, deliver something incredible to our clients?

When leaders fully embrace the concept of asking the right questions, the collective wisdom elevates to a new level. Communication is improved, and there is a greater commitment to the mission and movement toward alignment.

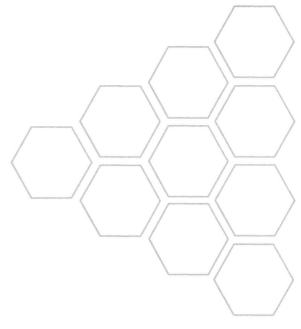

PART 4

THE SCIENTIFIC LEADER: WHERE DATA SCIENCE MEETS LEADERSHIP DECISIONS

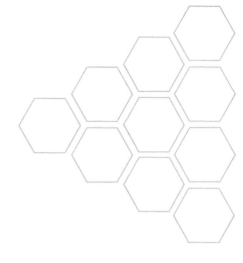

CHAPTER 21

PROBLEM #1: TURNOVER

*"To assure the prosperity of a firm a long-term strategy
and the turnover of key managers should be taken into account
from the standpoint of long-term consideration
and not from the monthly or quarterly flavors."*
– Masaaki Imai

One of the greatest problems leaders in both public and private sectors are faced with today is employee turnover. When companies invest in hiring, onboarding, training, and acquiring the assets necessary for their team members to do their jobs, it can be quite expensive. When those employees leave before they generate positive increases in production or revenue for the business, that negative net cost can be prohibitive. Some refer to this as "the cost of doing business." While that might be the case, leaders pursuing alignment in their organizations work to reduce this "cost" tremendously by attacking the underlying reasons why people leave and what could be done about it.

In aligned organizations, turnover is lower than in misaligned organizations due to strategies that are implemented *before* hiring individuals to fulfill necessary roles. Part of the hiring and onboarding process is to determine if, and how well, new hires buy into the mission and vision of the company, which is an indicator of how successful they will be within the organization. Some pre-hiring strategies also help determine if the new hires will like or fit in with the organization's culture.

Chris Price is the CEO of Price Leadership Group in Dallas. His company assists in the onboarding process. Simply put, his software measures the compatibility between employers and potential employees. The more compatible the match, the greater the likelihood of having a productive employee and a positive return on hire. If alignment is important, what's more critical than bringing in people who are aligned in the beginning? The degree to which their purpose is consistent with the mission and vision of the company provides a huge head start in ensuring alignment as they become productive in understanding the systems and expectations of their employment.

Discovering the "Why" of Turnover

Within those organizations that are misaligned or semi-aligned and experience an uncomfortable level of turnover, specific questions need to be asked to determine where the breakdown is and what can be done about it. Here are some questions that should provide sound answers for consideration before implementing new strategies:

- Is there a specific demographic of those who leave the organization?
- What are the common complaints among those who leave?
- Are more leaving from one department or division than another?
- Are people in certain roles leaving more often than others?
- Are the required resources limiting individuals' abilities to perform their roles to the best of their ability?
- Is there bi-directional communication happening where leaders are able to get the information they need to evaluate the reasons for turnover?
- Are individuals not being recognized for their efforts?
- Is the pay scale not matching the marketplace?

As an example, in the public sector, an assessment revealed that 18 percent of the employee base in the State of Arizona was turning over annually.[14] That's a significant number. Even more startling was that the percentage had increased for five straight years! Fourteen percent of that turnover fell into the realm of *voluntary* turnover. These are people who opt to leave to do other things versus being let go or retiring.

One of the reasons for this voluntary turnover in Arizona was that the base pay had not kept up with the market. As a straightforward step to resolve this issue, the governor increased the budget for compensation by 20 percent for many state employees. This decision quickly took care of what was seen as a systemic issue between public and private sector compensation. That was just one issue related to the turnover rate, but one that was easy to identify and relatively easy to resolve. This action was a step in the right direction. However, voluntary turnover has not changed much since the pay increase.

There will be times when financial compensation is not the challenge. There are other types of compensation that go a long way toward retaining employees. These include:

- Paid time off
- Preferred parking
- Travel vouchers
- Tickets to entertainment venues
- Gifts

Money is Not Always the Reason for Turnover

One of the more common reasons people leave their jobs is because of an unsatisfactory work environment. An example of this might be expecting workers to fulfill their roles and responsibilities but not making the proper tools available to them. This may include having them work with outdated software or equipment as an example. When systems and processes are cumbersome, frustration leads to job dissatisfaction. Employees relegated to a working environment devoid of tools necessary to get the job done effectively (equipment, training, and so on) feel they have been set up to fail or that the leaders don't care. The outcome is misalignment.

There could be a challenge with the processes required to keep work flowing. Bottlenecks in workflow are frustrating to all involved. It's up to the leaders in the organization to recognize those bottlenecks and help to alleviate them—removing the "rocks from the road" to the organization's goals.

Another reason for turnover among individuals is a lack of trust in the leadership or poor relationships with their bosses. When this happens, more time is spent complaining at the water cooler than getting work done. Therefore, when turnover is high or increasing, leaders should first take a look in the mirror and ask what they are doing that might be part of the problem. Most often, employees leave a *boss* versus leaving a job.

Going back to the state of Arizona, the evaluation determined that the average age of the workforce was in their mid- to late 40s. Because of this, leadership recognized that it was imperative to improve strategies to attract and retain younger state employees to lessen the impact of a large percentage of the workers retiring over the next 15 to 20 years. This requires different leadership skills than those that were effective when hiring the current workers. Efforts were put into play in Arizona to enhance the skills of those in, and moving into, leadership positions with the expectation of reducing turnover in the future.

Are Your Employees Playing the Job-Hopping Game?

In many industries in the private sector, it has become the norm to provide incentives to top talent to join organizations with so-called "signing bonuses" and other perks. These typically come with restrictions such as agreeing to work with the company for a period of two to five years and then not taking a similar position in a competing business. The thought behind this is to keep that top talent long enough to benefit from their expertise and efforts while preventing them from turning around and take their knowledge to the competition. Sadly, with many markets being so competitive, rather than becoming loyal to the company, many of these top workers simply operate like free agents, thus going to the highest bidder. Every two to five years, they seek out another opportunity with a more lucrative financial package. For those individuals, it can be *all* about the money. If the organization is not prepared to match the market value of the talent or create a working culture that promotes individual purpose, the outcome will be one of displacement.

Millennial Turnover

When it comes to compensation, the tide is turning with many employees, especially millennials. Yes, they want to be paid well for the work they do, but they are increasingly motivated by purpose. Over the last few decades, many individuals have become less interested in having a job they can retire from. Instead, there is a sense of wanting to be more strategic and "in control" of this significant portion of life.

Millennials have heard their parents lament over how much they didn't like their jobs, their bosses, or their co-workers. Whether directly or indirectly, those messages encourage young workers to follow their passions and find like-minded people with whom to work. They're advised: "Find something you care deeply about first. Then, seek out employment in that arena."

Those within or entering the workforce today lived through the crises related to the Great Recession of 2008. During that time, many realized they weren't going to be able to rely on the security of retiring from a company to which they dedicated their working careers. Millennials began realizing that it would be normal to have multiple employers over the course of their careers. This provides a distinctly different perspective on whether to stay or leave a job than their parents experienced.

Alignment Discourages Turnover

When the mission of the company is of specific interest to employees, money becomes less important. Rather, individuals want to participate in the success of the company mission. They need to feel their voices are heard and be recognized for their contributions to something larger than themselves. Their contributions and longevity with an organization are commensurate with how that organization meets their need to feel not just engaged but *aligned* with the overall purpose. Managing that type of mindset requires a very specific awareness and level of leadership skills. Engineers at Medtronic, regardless of age, are less apt to leave after attending its holiday party. As previously discussed, this alignment between individual purpose and corporate mission is a stronger retention tool than anything else.

Thus, the challenge in dealing with turnover is being able to adjust as a leader in such a way to get everyone in the organization contributing at their highest levels. These adjustments start with getting a sense of where any misalignment is and how to approach it in order to pinpoint prescriptive actions. Aligning an organization to its mission and vision while making certain all employees understand how they fit into it is critical for lowering turnover. This effort starts with developing the capacity of leaders to align *themselves* to the mission and to build a foundation of leadership skills in a purposeful manner. These skills are, but are not limited to:

1. **Effective listening**. This is the gateway to understanding individual purposes.
2. **Timely, purposeful recognition**. The acknowledgment of contributions is one thing. The storytelling and memorializing the accomplishment is very different. Items to be considered:
   a. Is the right person being recognized?
   b. Is this recognition an opportunity to reinforce the mission and vision?
   c. Is this the appropriate time to deliver this recognition? For example, during layoffs would not be an appropriate time.
3. **High level of self-awareness/personal accountability.** Employees see right through the leader who is not authentic. Leaders must walk the talk.

When leaders implement the strategies necessary to align their organizations, they consequentially reduce turnover and lower the cost of doing business.

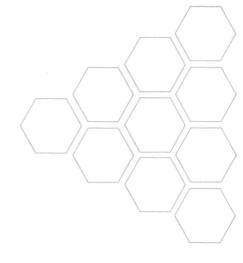

CHAPTER 22

PROBLEM #2: MISALIGNED EMPLOYEES

"Just as your car runs more smoothly and requires less energy to go faster and farther when the wheels are in perfect alignment, you perform better when your thoughts, feelings, emotions, goals, and values are in balance."
– Brian Tracy

When it comes to light that an individual within a team, a division, or organization is disengaged, this provides leaders with a great opportunity. The opportunity is to go deep into discovering what caused the disengagement. Doing so requires leaders to use well-developed communication skills.

Questions need to be asked, and leaders need to listen to what might be some tough answers.

Before communicating with those who are disengaged, leaders must ask themselves: "Am I willing to communicate in a manner that brings healthy conflict and allows me to be able to innovate and empower individuals?" If you're not ... if you're the type of leader who goes on a fault-finding mission rather than being focused on resolution, your mission needs to begin with the person in the mirror.

Focus on the Fuel

Great leaders don't get caught up in firefighting. Instead, they focus their attention on what fueled the fire and stopping it from spreading. They allow for the fact that a disengaged employee might be a change agent. Perhaps that employee sees something the leadership team hasn't seen and is just tired of banging their head against the wall, trying to force a resolution. It can never be assumed that the disengaged person is a "bad seed" who needs to be culled from the rest unless and until they've been given the opportunity to be heard. Often, "being heard" is enough for the disengaged party to re-engage—having had their say.

Part of leadership is having a strong belief that each person within the organization has value and wants to bring their A-game to the job. It's then up to the leader to find out what that is and help stoke the fires of engagement.

When Disengagement Occurs

When disengagement does occur, it's up to the leader to get to the bottom of it and determine a resolution. Some questions to ask immediately of disengaged employees include:

- What happened to cause their disengagement? Is the cause specifically work-related, or is there something personal going on?
- Is the situation that brought about disengagement temporary? If it's related to a current workload, perhaps a redistribution of the load is needed.
- Are there others who are also disengaging over this matter? Confer with other leaders in the organization to determine if there's a broader change in engagement.
- Is there a disconnect across teams or divisions? Does the resolution require a larger scale evaluation?
- If they were to suggest a different way of handling that issue, what would it be?
- Are they willing to work toward a positive solution to the disengagement?

Additionally, ask the disengaged employee to hold himself or herself accountable to at least trying to re-engage. Then, be prepared to hold yourself responsible for seeing that progress is made.

Acknowledge to the disengaged that you hear them and will get back to them about it. Create hope that re-engagement can occur. If it can't be addressed now, ask how the person can work within the situation.

Strong leaders want to learn if the cause of disengagement is something that's systemic or something they may have done, or a situation they've been involved in creating. The answers that are provided in honest, trusting, bi-directional communication can often lead to some introspection within the leadership of an entire organization.

Ideally, leaders are positively and openly communicating with individuals in such a way as to recognize disengagement immediately. Being proactive about discovering the cause is best for the organization *and* the individual.

How do you proactively read what's going on with employees around you?

- Get to know them as individuals.
- Build trust. Trust can prevent disengagement, but it will take time. This is where leaders match their words and deeds.
- Create an environment where individuals are comfortable to talk about what's going on, as opposed to being ostracized for pointing something out. This means encouraging honest conversations that can be had without repercussions. Whistleblowers are welcomed.

If the signs of disengagement are missed for any period of time, it's the leader's fault. Period. Or, if the signs are noted, yet not addressed, again, this is the fault of the leadership in allowing it to continue. This is where humility becomes a strength. Leaders who can humble themselves to take in any negatives that are presented will also likely be open to creative means of re-engaging individuals. The communication will be centered on resolving the issues rather than finding blame for what has led to them.

Miscommunication: The Leading Cause of Disengagement

In many cases, disengagement boils down to some sort of miscommunication or misunderstanding. For example, in some types of work such as public safety, or even in the building trades, there are certain aspects of business that are mandated for safety reasons. If something within the mandates is causing a challenge for someone, a deeper level of education on the matter may be all that is needed to resolve it. If those mandates remain an issue for the individual, the leader may need to change their focus to one of weighing the mandate against all of the positives the individual acknowledges within the organization.

An example of a disconnect occurred within a school district in the Minneapolis suburbs. The issue was that the demographics in the school district were changing rapidly. The graduating class at the high school level was 90 percent white, with a culture that had no challenges with the typical school day. Among the first graders in the district, approximately 40 percent were white. Families from different cultures were moving into the area, and their children had different needs. Among teachers about halfway along the educational spectrum, struggles were appearing related to lesson planning due to a need to allow middle school children time to pray at midday.

In all school districts, there are layers of responsibility. At the higher level, district plans are developed. They are then passed along through the layers to principals, who would then drive the mission of the plans down to the teachers, administrative team, janitors, and cafeteria workers, so everyone is focusing their efforts on the same mission.

In one instance, a principal spoke up at a meeting, indicating that the plan that was created wouldn't work for the children in his school. They had some specific challenges that required a different type of approach. In fact, he was so disengaged from the plan that he had developed his own. The disconnect was that his plan didn't match the mission and vision of the district at large. Rather than calling him out as a rogue, the leaders discerned that they hadn't communicated well bi-directionally to gather input from all the principals *before* completing the development of the "district" plan. With input from all of the principals, modifications were made to the plan that re-engaged those at all levels and created alignment to the mission. Moreover, this principal was lauded for creativity and asked to participate in a task force to solve asymptomatic district challenges compromised by herd mentality.

Is Re-engagement the Answer?

The worst scenario in terms of employment issues is the employee who quits but does not leave. They still show up most days, collect their paychecks, and take their vacation time, but their work becomes sub-par. They may talk about how the grass is greener on the other side of the fence, but they're not motivated enough to climb the fence. This may be your C-player who scales down to the D and F area. When review periods approach, they may scale back up to the C area just enough to meet expectations in order not to be let go. Generally, they are not getting the job done. They have checked out mentally and emotionally. Unfortunately, they are good at finding others they can bring over to their camp, and their malaise becomes like a cancer.

The challenge for leaders is to identify who these individuals are and quickly decide whether or not they can be turned around. If there's no way to re-engage them, leaders must help them to find something else to do outside the organization (termination) or redirect them to a position within the organization that might be a better fit for them.

Keeping them might not be the best idea, though. That is because those who hide within an organization—not performing at their best—are not likely to become highly contributing members of the team in a different position. It rarely happens that someone who performs at a low level all of a sudden changes direction and becomes the fantastic employee everyone wants on their team. More often than not, this individual should be shown the door. In doing so, leadership may be doing that person a favor—giving them an opportunity to find an organization better suited to them. They will certainly be benefitting the company by making this change, and this action can build trust and reaffirm the mission.

After cutting out the cancer, the leader's next challenge is in re-engaging all the others that person impacted. Identify what drove the low-level behaviors and address those factors. Even after the disengaged are gone, some of the cultural seeds they planted (or fertilized) might continue to grow unless and until they are addressed. By constantly soliciting input, leaders can tremendously reduce the amount of disengagement their organization experiences. Remember, strong leaders continually ping those in the organization for feedback related to strategy, structure, and culture.

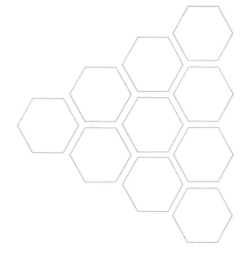

CHAPTER 23

PROBLEM #3: AMBIGUITY

"There is no greater impediment to the advancement of knowledge than the ambiguity of words."
– Thomas Reid

C lear, concise messages across the board are required for alignment in an organization. At least, that is the ideal. However, ambiguity can occur even in aligned organizations. This could be a function of message attenuation or conduit distortion. Simply put, the message needs to be reinforced, or distractions need to be minimized. That is simply because each human being operates at their own frequency.

Mission statements and strategic plans can have conflicting topics or be interpreted differently down the line. An example of this is when an organization has an objective to gain market share and maintain an average selling price. If you are a market leader and you are trying to gain market share, you may have to lower prices or make other concessions to do so. This is especially the case in areas where customers have comparable competitive options. Lower pricing is the most common lure when product quality and value propositions are similar.

Part of the price reduction strategy is to use the price lever to gain market share and tie up clients in long-term contracts. That, in turn, conflicts with maintaining an average selling price. So, how do you manage these two things at the same time when they are in direct conflict with each other? You can't. Your teams will vacillate between one and the other. There will be no consistency of effort. Therefore, ambiguity becomes the problem. It creates all kinds of chasms within the organization. It is incumbent upon leaders to minimize the distraction factor in messaging and reinforce the mission.

An example of this comes from Starbucks. In April of 2018, two African American men were sitting at a table in Starbucks in Philadelphia, waiting for a friend. They had not made any purchases. The store manager told them they couldn't stay if they didn't make a purchase. They refused to leave, again, because they were waiting for someone. The store manager called the police, and the police removed the men—in hand-cuffs. This experience was far different from what the leadership and organization wanted to have happen. The experience of these two men started a wildfire of negative media attention—all from the action of a single Starbucks employee who stepped outside the company's mission.

Starbucks' mission statement is all about the customer experience: "To inspire and nurture the human spirit—one person, one cup and one neighborhood at a time." Their number one value is creating a culture of warmth and belonging, where everyone is welcome. The incident in Philadelphia demonstrated that there was a disconnect or lack of buy-in with this manager.

The CEO of Starbucks called the situation "reprehensible." He personally flew to Philadelphia to apologize, vowing to work with all store managers and employees to address any "unconscious bias" throughout the chain. He then met with various community leaders in an attempt to bridge the gap created by this situation.

Starbucks also closed all 15,000 locations for a half-day to address this situation with all employees. They created training for how to specifically address this type of situation in the future and worked to get buy-in from all individuals within the organization so this situation would not happen again. The loss of millions of dollars in revenue, the media storm, and re-training expenses might have been avoided had clear, concise direction been provided in the company's strategic plan—and had they driven it down through the organization to get buy-in at all levels.

Unfortunately, Starbucks had a situation after the 2018 event where it could have lived up to its mission and missed the mark. In response to racial unrest after police killings of Black Americans, some employees wanted to wear Black Lives Matter shirts in their locations in response to the need for greater racial equity in the aftermath of the George Floyd killing. Starbucks' leadership declined the request, telling employees that they couldn't wear such attire for fear of how it would be perceived by customers. This decision diverted from their statements regarding equity and sensitivity, angering customers. Leadership backtracked quickly in response to the blowback from that decision. They've since created shirts that are fairly broad in terms of demonstrating Starbucks' position on equity and inclusivity, and allowed the wearing of BLM shirts only temporarily until the new shirts arrived. They had a chance to lead in this area and live up to their mission, "To inspire and nurture the human spirit—one person, one cup and one neighborhood at a time." However, they instead decided to steer away from it. Only after pressure did they come back to it. It takes "consistent" and "intentional" work to build and maintain alignment to mission and vision at all levels. Just because training was completed doesn't mean alignment is ingrained.

Deliver Messages the Way Others Need to Hear Them

When situations are confusing or emotions are high, it's likely that individuals will deliver the company message the way that's most comfortable for *them*, rather than how leadership wanted it done. The focus becomes one of "saying it how I want to say it" rather than how the recipient receives the message.

Part of the role of the leader is to make sure that there is no room for ambiguity—to avoid situations that can send individuals chasing their tails to achieve the impossible or, worse, doing nothing because of lack of a clear direction. These activities often lead to employee burnout.

Instead, mission statements and strategic plans should be cohesive, prescriptive, and have *very* clear messages. When confusing or unusual situations arise, the mission statement is the compass by which all judgments are made and actions taken. The mission can create an accountability system when no one is around to reinforce the message.

Customer-Focused Mission Statements

The best mission statements remain customer-focused. Conversely, a mission statement that includes increasing market share is very inward-focused. When customers see that type of mission statement, they will likely wonder what is in it for them to get involved with that organization.

Your mission statement defines who you are and what you are about, while the vision is what the world will look like when these things come to fruition. Your strategic plan is the roadmap that gets you there. The goal of the strategic plan is to show the individuals and teams within the organization how to deliver on the mission statement that is customer-focused.

When strategic plans are not clear enough to get everyone flying in formation, and at the correct course heading, that's where ambiguity comes in. The role of the leader is to encourage feedback on those strategic plans, to recognize problems within them, and then to fix those problems—to keep steering the formation toward the intended destination. Consider the journey of the Canadian goose once again. Flying in formation embodies strategy, structure, and culture. The strategy is to conserve as much energy as possible on the way to the destination, as well as allow the geese to keep track of each other. The structure is to form a V-like shape to enhance ergonomics and accountability. The fact that the geese frequently switch between leading and trailing positions, so that no single goose becomes overly tired, makes it clear that no bird is more important than the next. As each takes the lead, the direction toward the mission and vision remains the same. Leaders can learn a lot from this species!

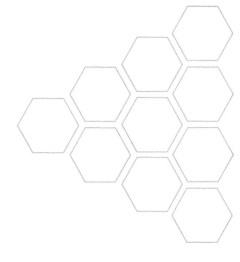

CHAPTER 24

PROBLEM #4: POOR SIGNAL ATTENUATION

"Intensity, like signal strength, will generally fall off with distance from the source."
– Charles Francis Richter

One of the biggest challenges to accountability is the culture of an organization. If you have a culture that is lacking accountability, it can be difficult to change. When the culture, instead, is one of consistency across the leadership team, as well as down throughout the organization, the strength of any message can be enhanced. There are three buckets of aligned leadership plans and practice that need to be considered:

Group/Team: This is your functional team, usually the higher-level leaders who are effectively communicating in every direction.

Inter-Group: This relates to your leaders and individuals who work across teams, departments, or divisions for the benefit of the larger organization. Again, the communication is multi-directional. We often see this in matrix-managed organizations.

Individual: This involves the daily interactions that connect all levels and groups for the common goal—the mission and vision of the organization. Individual purpose, consistent with mission and vision, equals true alignment.

It's critical for there to be consistency across all three of those buckets for an organization to become aligned. A culture of accountability brings the mission to life. In aligned organizations, this accountability is most frequently to all stakeholders. This was demonstrated in a 1980s cop show called "Hill Street Blues." It espoused officer safety. After every briefing for the day, the sergeant would conclude with, "Let's be careful out there." This was his way of reaffirming the mission.

Eliminating the Disconnect Between Performance and Outcome

When the level of performance is considered "good enough," individuals will settle into a spirit of, "That's how we have always done it," and resist change. When organizations reach a point where contributions at that level are no longer meeting their needs, it's time for the leaders to drive greater levels of accountability. Their job becomes one of eliminating the disconnect between performance and outcome when the business is either losing market share or attempting to gain greater share.

In other words, the leadership needs to specifically redefine what winning is and establish what the metrics of performance are for each individual. The expectations need to be laid out with a vision of how everyone must come together to create this overall win for the organization. Winning, in this case, will involve specifically hitting the targets and goals that have been established as success factors.

The key to the success of instigating such change is to not only make everyone aware of the new strategy, but to get buy-in at such a degree that the message is both constant and consistent, thus avoiding attenuation. Attenuation is defined by *Merriam-Webster* as "the reduction of the force, effect or value of something." In the case of electrical current, it is when the amplitude of a current lessens the farther it gets from its source. Within organizations, attenuation happens when there is a lack of consistency in messaging and actions, starting with the leadership.

Cascading Consistent Messaging

Part of the role of a leader is to be clear on the direction of the organization and buy-in from everyone involved. This creates a cascade of consistent messaging throughout the organization at the leadership level, within divisions, teams, and in the hearts and minds of individuals. Without attention to this aspect of business, by the time the message gets to the individual contributor from the CEO, it has passed through the hands or mouths of several leaders. What you want to make sure of is that the message does not get diluted on the way; therefore, strengthening the signal and preventing attenuation becomes paramount.

As you get that word out and measure performance against the plan, you will see clearly whether or not the delivery of the message is strong enough and, possibly, where the weak links exist. When the scope of and responsibilities related to what success looks like are clear and strong, individuals often feel personally responsible for the success of the organization and many times will be compelled to deliver at a higher level of performance.

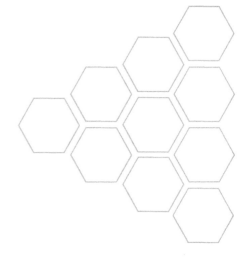

CHAPTER 25

PROBLEM #5: NOT KNOWING STAKEHOLDERS

"In a free enterprise, the community is not just another stakeholder in business, but is in fact the very purpose of its existence."
– Jamsetji Tata

Who are your stakeholders? Who are the stakeholders of your direct reports, besides you? Does everyone within your purview know to whom they are accountable within the organization? Do they understand that they're accountable not just for their daily work, but to the mission and vision of the organization? It's up to leaders to ensure that these questions are answered and recapped in communication regularly.

A school district in the United States held a leadership team meeting to discuss ways to improve test scores and graduation rates. The solution quickly pointed to identifying all stakeholders. This list was hamstrung by limited scope, and it was believed that the stakeholders were only those people who were seen during the course of the workday. Needless to say, it had to be expanded to include the broader community and subsequent generations.

360 Degrees of Accountability

It's imperative that each member of the team understands there are 360 degrees of accountability. Their actions have the potential to impact every aspect of the business. Each is, at least, accountable to a boss, peers, customers, shareholders, and the community.

When leaders do a good job of establishing due north from a directional standpoint, everyone knows where they are going. When leaders do a *really* good job of explaining how everyone contributes to the direction the organization is going and how they will be measured, that becomes the guiding light. This removes ambiguity and strengthens the message signal. Stakeholder clarity, coupled with accountability, translates to alignment.

Know Your People!

When a leader communicates with others, it's valuable to keep in mind the importance of knowing them as individuals. Leaders should want to know the dynamics of each person's role, their daily tasks, who they report to, what the work environment is, and so on. They will be prepared to ask, "Where do you want to go, and how will you get there?" and "What's keeping you from accomplishing that in an expedient manner?" Leaders who ask these questions and listen to the answers will find gaps in the alignment of the organization and then be able to analyze them and provide prioritized solutions.

Note that the answers to resolving issues may not be clear cut. Let's say the challenge is related to what the individual refers to as outdated software. The obvious solution might be to consider upgrading the software. However, the underlying issue may not be the software at all. It may be that the training on the use of the software has been insufficient. It could be that the software in use isn't the right one for the need. It could be that the processes tracked by the software need to be improved. Sound like Pandora's box? It can be. The point of the exercise, though, is for leaders to continually seek out ways to improve the organization according to its mission and vision through the stakeholders. Consider the school district that expanded its list of stakeholders to include law enforcement. The outcome was improved communication between the high school and police department. This effective communication led to a student planning a horrific act being apprehended before a catastrophic outcome, and a broader sense of alignment was achieved!

When all stakeholders are on the same page with the mission and plan of the organization, there is little question of what needs to be done or who will do it. When in doubt, everyone looks to the mission, vision, strategic plan, and their job description. That's what success looks like within an organization.

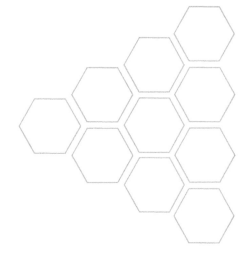

CHAPTER 26

PROBLEM #6: THE AUTOCRATIC LEADER

"In a democracy, there will be more complaints but less crisis, in a dictatorship more silence but much more suffering."
– Amit Kalantri

When leaders rely on the authority of their position to push their agendas down through the ranks, this creates problems. They have little personal influence. Their "influence" comes from the position and any level of respect that it generates. That style of leadership goes directly against the nine pillars of leadership that drive today's most aligned organizations.

That being said, there are types of organizations in which autocratic leadership is valuable. There are some fields in which such a structure is beneficial, such as paramilitary organizations. There are very specific procedures and rules that must be adhered to in certain scenarios such as with a house fire, domestic call, car chase, or an active shooter because if they're not, people can be severely injured or die.

However, even paramilitary organizations need empowerment. Whether consciously or subconsciously, individuals within the organization need to keep the overall mission and vision in mind and act accordingly. Let's say that a police department has an increase in community involvement as part of its mission and vision. When an officer is called about a group of kids disturbing someone's peace, the response could either be authoritarian or one of "peacemaker." A video of an officer playing basketball with a group of kids he was called on to investigate went viral. It demonstrated a positive way of engaging the kids while explaining how to keep the peace with neighbors.

It's up to the leader to understand whether or not autocratic leadership is necessary in their organization. Note: There's limited need for it in business organizations beyond what might be dictated by OSHA. That limited need shouldn't occur often. When leaders are managing well, most people will arrive at these things on their own. However, sometimes macro events take place that require immediate pivots to autocracy for the immediate future, but that should be a rarity.

Traits of the Autocratic Leader

This book is not intended to explain why someone becomes an autocratic leader. Instead, let's better understand some of the traits of one so we can recognize them.

- Need for attention
- Desire for complete control
- Doesn't take feedback well
- Is "The Oracle of Information"
- Leads through fear and intimidation
- Looks to place blame
- Takes credit for positive outcomes

Sadly, most autocratic leaders in business have a belief that they are the only ones who understand the big picture. They believe they are "dictating" what is right for the company. The direction of the organization is articulated, and there is this effect of rolling a ball down a hill where it crushes everything on its way—especially the desires of others in the organization to offer ideas and strategies for improvement. However, in instances where resources are limited, or there are time constraints, a direct approach may be necessary. Otherwise, the most effective style is to imbue individual purpose in concert with the mission.

How Others Respond to the Autocratic Leader

There will always be those who respond well enough to the autocratic style of leadership in that they just want to be told what to do and not carry the burden of responsibility beyond fulfilling their basic job duties. These people cannot be motivated to perform at a higher level. In fact, they may even underperform or cause harm to the organization through their allegiance to pleasing that leader rather than working for the good of the organization.

The willingness of employees to tolerate the autocratic leader has diminished. In general, society has instilled in today's workers that they have value, and that value should be appreciated. Work environments should be considered safe physically, mentally, and emotionally. Autocratic leaders tend not to consider how the work environment impacts the performance levels of individuals. In this case, unions, affinity groups, human resources, and whistleblowers give voice to the unheard.

With an autocratic leadership style, there is no empowerment. Without empowerment, you lose opportunities to energize the organization. People will feel that they have been told what to do. When they do get recognized for their work, it is disingenuous because all they have done is what they have been told to do. Therefore, we are recognizing the person who gave them their orders for the results that were generated. In essence, those in leadership are really recognizing themselves for choosing what should be done and then getting others to do it.

Effective Leaders

Effective leaders do not want to dictate. They do not want to micro-manage. They want to explain the direction of the organization, get buy-in, and let those who are closest to the work that needs to be done determine *how* to accomplish the mission. The "leader" then becomes the "cheerleader," encouraging the teams and divisions. More importantly, they continually monitor the strength of harmony between strategy, structure, and culture.

Part of the responsibility of an effective leader is to keep themselves out of the job of making decisions on anything beyond mission and strategy. Clear messaging and empowerment allow leaders to be more strategic, and the implementation is done by the teams and individuals.

When leaders meddle in the finer points of implementation, it stagnates employee growth and development while eroding trust. This was seen in the past at Medtronic. There was a belief among those at the most senior levels that sales executives needed to establish relationships with existing customers, even when strong relationships already existed between the reps and clients. The perception was that if the execs had deep relationships with clients, they couldn't be fired. This was ludicrous because the executives were retracing the steps already taken by the reps. They were undermining the trust of those reps, allowing for paranoia to creep in as they questioned if they were about to be replaced.

The best leaders drive decision making down through the organization in order to get faster and better decisions. Some leaders disagree with this strategy because they feel it will make them obsolete or irrelevant. Not true. It just changes the value of their skillsets. Leaders need, instead, to be able to encourage innovation from those closest to the actions that are being required.

When the right people with the right skills are in the right roles, the best answers will come from those people who are closest to the work that must be done. Many leaders are reluctant to do that. In other words, they feel good when someone comes into their office and asks permission to do something. There's a euphoric feeling of power when that happens. Instead, that leader should realize that either the message is not clear or else a culture of "Mother, may I?" permeates. It can feel good to have answers for people, but today's best leaders understand the value in helping others to come up with their own answers. Instead of being reactive with answers, great leaders draw out responses from others by saying, "You know, I am not really sure, what do you think?" Asking questions like that generates more ideas to explore than just what the leader has to offer. When others contribute ideas that become part of the solution or action that must be taken, there is an inherent sense of empowerment and accountability that drives performance levels up.

As an effective leader, it's important to be able to recognize autocratic tendencies in yourself and adjust accordingly. It's also important to recognize those tendencies in direct reports and be able to guide them in how to handle communication down the line. Helping others understand the value of empowerment by eliminating autocratic tendencies will improve the overall performance of the organization and contribute to sustainable alignment.

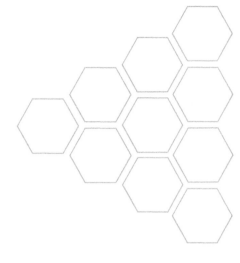

CHAPTER 27

PROBLEM #7: INCONSISTENCY IN COMMUNICATIONS

"Consistency is the true foundation of trust.
Either keep your promises or do not make them."
– Roy T. Bennett

E dward George Bulwer Lytton is famed for writing, "The pen is mightier than the sword." His point was that communication is more effective at producing change than violence with weapons will ever be. While there's no need for weapons in today's business world, effective communication is a requirement for the success of all organizations.

When we think about communication, the words being used must be evaluated—weighed, if you will. People have become hyper-sensitive to how ideas are interpreted, and words cannot be left unspoken. In fact, they may need to be spoken in many different ways. The best leaders understand that messages must be delivered in the language of the listener—at a frequency they can receive.

Each person's understanding of words comes from their own perspectives and can vary greatly. There's a story about two men on their first visit to Chicago that demonstrates this point. Having some time on their hands, these two men took a walk around the city. When asked by another person about their impressions of the city, their answers were very different. One stated that Chicago was beautiful. He very much appreciated the beautiful buildings and parks. The other stated that he didn't like the city at all. All he saw were factors that led to having a high crime rate. These two people shared the same walk! How is it that they had different answers? It might be helpful for you to know that one of the people was an architect. The other was a police officer.

Because of how experience and perspective influence everyone's understanding and interpretation of words, great leaders work on becoming multi-lingual. Becoming so requires dedication and practice, but great leaders can speak "fellow leader." They can speak "line manager," "accounting," "sales" and "warehouse." Each has its own distinct frequency by which messages are interpreted.

The Importance of Tying All Communication to the Mission and Vision

The most critical aspect of effective business communication is that it is consistent with the overall mission and vision of the organization. When the mission and vision are clear, they become the foundation of a common language and frequency for everyone involved. That being said, leaders can never assume employees will understand that their messages are consistent with the mission and vision. They must continually *state* that their messages are in line with the overall mission and vision, and then demonstrate *how* they are in line.

Compare this to a sales call where the salesperson simply states, "This is the best widget in the industry." Without backup proof of the statement, it does little other than creating doubt in the mind of the buyer. Leaders need to consistently back up their communications—all the way back to the company's mission and vision—every time! The goal is to provide clarity and eliminate doubt. When doubt creeps in, interpretations vary, and conflict arises.

When leaders either are not clear, or they send conflicting messages, they create the opportunity for employees to pick and choose which message or leader to follow. It's been known to happen that people without the designation or job description of "leader" are viewed by co-workers as informal leaders. These are people whose opinions are paid attention to within the rank and file. When informal leaders are identified, it's important to know what they espouse. One employee may go with one strategy and another employee with another, and these conflicting strategies will cause a decrease in overall performance. There will be infighting. It's bound to happen that people will join various camps with differing beliefs from what they're supposed to be doing.

In situations where more than one message needs to be delivered, it's up to the leaders to determine and emphasize priorities. As an example, if a new strategic plan has three parts, the leader is responsible for explaining the three parts and how they work together toward the end goal. If necessary, the leader may break down each step, explaining why they must be accomplished in phases and how team members can mentally or physically prepare for each next step. When strategic plans are made clear, it's so much easier to get both buy-in and results.

> To enhance communication with all team members in the Mountain region at Medtronic, we held weekly group teleconferences. Representatives from different departments at corporate were also asked to attend. This way, when a question arose about something related to HR, the person from that department could provide an answer on the spot. A representative from finance was also on the calls to provide the latest reports on progress within the region. With this simple adjustment in communication, we eliminated the morale-defeating delays that occur when questions crop up and the answer is, "I don't know. Let me get back to you on that."

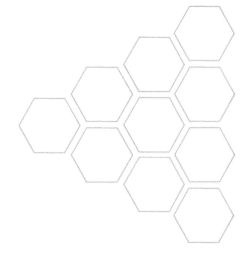

CHAPTER 28

PROBLEM #8:
RESOURCE ALLOCATION

*"When resources become skimpy, human beings don't suddenly
cooperate to conserve what's left. They fight to the last scrap for
possession of a diminishing resource."*
– Deepak Chopra

While most people in an organization are likely to agree on the value of proper resource allocation, some may balk at a change in the allocation of *their* resources. With a clear mission and vision and a proper level of buy-in to it, any pushback on changes in allocation will be better understood. In misaligned organizations where many have placed their focus on their own fiefdoms—not considering the overall success of the organization—egos can get in the way of forward progress. Leaders will need to help those people look at the business differently, perhaps even breaking down structures that are held together by nothing more than those egos. The mission and vision outline what is best for the company, and everything else must align with it.

Once a strategic direction is established within an organization, the allocation of materials and efforts must match it. For example, if it is determined wise to move one particular product to the forefront of the company's offerings, resources in everything from research and development to training to marketing must be adjusted to fulfill that decision. When corporate direction has been established, and resources are not allocated in like manner, this is the precursor to misalignment. Ensuing water cooler conversations point out the inconsistencies, leading to this runaway train called, "message distortion."

Setting a goal for achievement without the follow-up of resources is setting people up to fail. When that project fails, it makes other departments, divisions, and individuals nervous about the commitment of the organization and can cause discord. This can result in territorialism, segmentation, and keeping people from working toward the broader goals of the organization. If market data supports a trend that's consistent with the growth of a product line, it would behoove leadership to allocate resources accordingly. This is similar to the championship Chicago Bulls referenced earlier getting the ball in the hands of their best shooter as much as possible. It simply increases the likelihood of winning.

In the example of Lexmark used earlier in the book, consideration of where trends were going made the spinoff a good decision. Rather than being caught up in legacy products, IBM went from requiring 240 signatures to launch a new product to only eight. It was able to reduce costs, increase speed to market, and generate higher profits.

Allocation is the Responsibility of Leadership

Knowing how, when, and where to allocate resources is a leadership responsibility. Staying on top of trends requires constant attention in three areas of business:

Market research data: This includes keeping a close watch on the competition—paying attention to both their successes and failures. Market receptivity to competitive products and its messaging is valuable data.

Open lines of communication within the company: This means listening to what the frontline employees or teams are seeing and hearing from the customers. Having the means for the sales and customer service teams to deliver messages up through the organization is critical to resource allocation and product development.

Direct feedback from customers: Surveys, focus groups, and phone calls are all tremendous ways of interacting directly with customers. The sales and service teams do this all the time. When leadership follows suit, great ideas and strategies can be discovered. A simple question to get customers talking is, "If we could wave a magic wand and create the ideal product/service for you, what would it look like?" This can go a long way toward helping companies plan for positive resource allocation. It has a way of endearing the customer whose input is sought.

The most effective allocation of resources can only be planned with proper input. It's up to the leadership of the organization to create an environment where they can gain the most feedback about where to guide the company next.

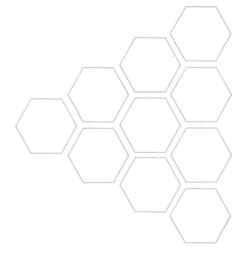

CHAPTER 29

PROBLEM #9:
STIFLING CREATIVITY

*"Don't mistake activity for productivity. Creativity is
productivity—it just doesn't feel like it at first."*
– Gino Wickman

Innovative work must be encouraged for *every* department
and individual. Companies that delegate creativity to
a single department, let's say Research and Development,
stagnate the generation of new ideas, thus going against the
adage "two heads are better than one." Ultimately, the creation of new products may fall to a single department, but
the generation of ideas that impact the organization and its
stakeholders cannot.

When people are passionate about their work and excited about the mission and vision of the organization, they are more likely to come up with creative ideas to benefit the organization and its customers. When leadership is open and bi-directional communication is in place, the volume of ideas around products, processes, and strategy can be staggering. The defeatist attitude of "what's the use" is eliminated. The experience instead becomes one of "I can make a difference!"

> After trust had been established and communication opened in the Mountain Region at Medtronic, we were able to eliminate some bad habits. One such habit was that representatives would often stockpile inventory to the point where some of it would become obsolete before it was used.
>
> One of my team members suggested the creation of a central locker where inventory could be readily accessible by all—rather than waiting for shipments from headquarters.
>
> Other team members got creative with the development of printed materials for doctors to provide patients after Medtronic devices had been implanted. Those materials answered, "What happens next?"—the most frequently asked questions by patients. The creativity involved in the development of these materials made life better for everyone involved—the patients, doctors, and representatives.

Creativity Leads to Productivity

It is often said that millennials are a different breed when it comes to what they do for a living. They want to do "cool" work and participate in something that changes the world for the better. They look at products and services in terms of whether or not they appeal to their values and vote with their feet. Simon Sinek says, "When people are emotionally invested, they want to contribute." If they find that anything within the organization doesn't match their values, they will seek employment elsewhere or start their *own* businesses.

This is not to say that other generations are less creative or value creativity less, but they're more settled into their careers and less likely to take new risks. Leaders usually know the people on their teams who think outside the box. Wise leaders become effective at drawing those people out. When leadership encourages the development of creative ideas, people respond.

Not every idea will have great value, but all ideas should be recognized. What gets recognized gets repeated. By tapping into the creative resources of everyone on the team, organizations encourage innovative work within alignment guard rails. This can be done by simply asking everyone leaders encounter, from their peers to the janitor, "What do you think about _____?" Or stating, "I'd like to hear your opinion of _____."

Some leaders like the idea of presenting a challenge, such as, "In order to achieve a higher profit margin, which affects each of us directly, we need to reduce expenses in the area of _____." Everyone is then encouraged to make suggestions for doing so. This goes beyond the black hole of a suggestion box. Wise leaders put a procedure in place for taking in ideas, considering them from different angles, and either requesting additional input or providing feedback on them in a timely manner. Leadership must be prepared to express an understanding of how each person's perspective on the topic is different and very much appreciated.

Transparency Leads to Creativity

Another way to encourage creativity across all levels is to require that issues, opportunities, or procedures get examined or re-examined on a consistent basis. An example might be with a CEO who challenges each member of the leadership team to bring a list of issues or opportunities that have been brought forth within their area to the next leadership team meeting. One of the ideas will be reviewed and discussed by the entire leadership team. Or, perhaps the CEO names a specific issue around which they'd like to have more discussion. It could be something more granular than profit margin—possibly some-thing around a broader strategy that impacts the organization as a whole. When the results of such a commiseration are positive, strategies and ground rules would be set for how the leadership team can cascade this through to teams. Down at the first-level teams, this could become a brainstorming session.

The team lead could say there's an interest in gathering ideas from the broader organization to consider the issue and see what solution is devised. That session may bring forth some leads to dig deeper into and connect with other departments to discuss the issue across teams at the ground level. A process would be established where the teams come back with concepts and then roll those up to the next level above them. There may be some connection points at higher levels that require commu-nication across teams before getting to top leadership, which might hone the ideas further. The outcome is cross-functional collaboration to solve a broader issue that could lead to higher profits and require appropriate recognition. The by-product is innovation, which is found at the intersection of creativity and empowerment.

A specific solution doesn't need to be had. However, identifying where the problems are, their significance, and opportunities to remove them can be brought up with top leadership. Conclusions from that type of meeting can then go down the chain again, and the process can start over until the best ideas rise to the top and have strategic plans built around them.

At Medtronic, I started a Representative Advisory Council to identify informal leaders and give them a way to espouse their ideas. It allowed me visibility into their capabilities and helped me identify how they could handle broader responsibilities within the organization. Ideas from the higher leadership teams could be vetted with this group, and bi-directional communication was its foundation.

This was also a way to recognize my team members for their contributions. Different people were invited to be on the council each year. They would have the opportunity to meet with key leaders from other divisions within the organization and learn more about the big picture.

We met quarterly, sometimes in fun locations within the region. Other times we brought them into the corporate office, combining work and play into the meetings to further develop relationships and trust.

The Benefits of Creativity

Regardless of whether monumental change happens from this one process, there are a number of benefits.

- A culture and process for creative ideas gets seeded throughout the organization, which can then grow and develop.
- Employees feel valued for their opinions and empowered to express ideas from their point of view.
- A culture of learning and questioning, without judgment or prejudice, is established, which will keep the organization fresher and increase trust.
- Any solutions that come forth from the process will, inherently, have people who hold themselves and one another more accountable to its success as they were part of the process.
- There's stronger trust in a leadership team that doesn't portray itself as having all the answers.
- Recognition of a breakthrough solution that advances the mission is truly energizing to the organization.

The more that leadership, at all levels, requires input and insight from everyone in the organization, the better off they will be.

Strategies for Encouraging Creativity

For those who are reluctant to bring forth comments in front of a group, even their own team, individual conversations might be needed. While somewhat time-consuming, having leaders interact with others at that level creates a higher level of trust and openness. Conscientious leaders provide a mechanism for all voices to be heard. After all, why would any leader want to limit idea generation to the ones who *talk* the most versus those who *think* the most?

The organization would need to establish a means of capturing the ideas. One method of capturing ideas is to set up an internal or Dropbox-type folder that everyone can add to—with an option for anonymity for the more private people in the group. Benchmarks would be established to measure the result of the creative ideas. Parties would be designated to evaluate the ideas by a certain date and time. Everyone who submits an idea is recognized, even if their idea has no immediate value to the organization. This idea might trigger other thoughts that get the organization closer to real innovation. The University of Wisconsin - Stout in Menomonie, Wisconsin has perfected this with a handful of axioms:

- No bad ideas
- Everyone can participate
- All suggestions are transparent
- Anonymity is permitted
- Leadership visibility and sentiment is memorialized
- Transparent economic feasibility analysis
- Recognition is mandatory

Creativity cannot be demanded; it can only be encouraged. It is measured by its result, which is innovation. Innovation is the antecedent of creativity.

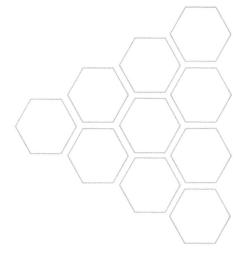

CHAPTER 30

PROBLEM #10: LACK OF BEST PRACTICES

"Innovation and best practices can be sown throughout an organization—but only when they fall on fertile ground."
– Marcus Buckingham

Leaders must first demonstrate that they are aligned within the organization before they can expect others to become so. The job of leaders is to set examples for others to follow and to expand the possibilities of the fulfillment of the mission and vision of the organization.

When leaders do not display that they are aligned, no one else will believe in the importance of doing so. Employees say,

"You want me to give *my* best work, but you're not looking for ways to continuously improve the organization. Why is it all on me?" If employees don't perform, they are to blame, but if, "We're all in this together," wouldn't we all be trying to find better ways to do this—including looking outside our organization?

The most critical job of leaders when it comes to best practices is to first admit there's room for improvement. There's a mixed message from some organizations that strive to hire the best and the brightest yet fail to establish a culture of continually seeking new and better ways to perform. In these instances, what's the motivation for the best and brightest to stay and grow?

When wins don't come, teams that commit to best practices work collectively to understand where the gaps are. There's validation for the positive work that is done along with a request for everyone to seek to identify gaps, come up with solutions to address them, and then make progress toward success once again.

Foster a Learning Organization

Within the realm of effective communication, it's the leaders' job to communicate what has been done, how strategic plans have been developed, and the impact on both employees and customers of performing at the highest levels. An organization that embraces best practices is a learning organization that has a culture of continuous improvement. Even when various projects are successful, there are areas where everyone can learn and further improve.

Best practices are found at the intersection of accountability and creativity, and teamwork is what takes this notion to the next level. Bi-directional communication of best practices leads to forming a culture of continuous improvement, which speaks volumes to employees. Think of it this way: Leaders are asking employees to provide their best work. When the employees don't see where the organization is trying to do *its best*, it becomes easy to perform in a subpar fashion.

Best practices require diligent benchmarking—both internal and external to the organization. Sometimes trial and error are required if there are minimal sources for gleaning benchmark data. The efforts behind the establishment of best practices go a long way in terms of creating a culture of continuous improvement.

Nick Saban, head coach of Alabama's Crimson Tide, is famous for creating indomitable teams. He has six national championships under his belt.

His general philosophy is that there's only one way to do things: the correct way. His focus is to determine the correct way to play the game against each opponent, and then train for it. His players train and prepare to such a high level that the games become predictable. Each player practices to be able to do their individual jobs very well for the entire 60 minutes of each game. They have a plan for how to play strong through the fourth quarter. I learned about this from Richard Levy, who was the vice president of finance at Medtronic when I started there. He graduated from the University of Alabama and is a die-hard fan.

When we first met, we invested two solid days together to develop the framework for how the Mountain Region of

Medtronic could excel. We put together a game plan to drive decision-making down through the ranks; to empower each member of the team, and to determine what to measure. Our plan was developed to an excruciating level of granularity upon which my team and I built structure and processes. And it worked beautifully!

Organizations cannot measure how well they are performing until they perform. As progress is made, you must continually seek out ways to improve. To develop best practices, leaders need to determine, through communication, the correct way to create alignment and then turn it into a habit. Everyone in the organization must remain open to ways to improve those habits. Having a productive morning leads to a productive day, and best practices are reflected every step of the way.

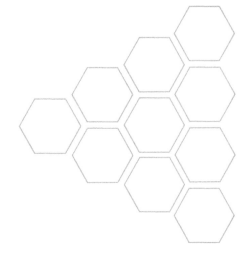

CONCLUSION

B ill George, Professor of Management Practice at Harvard Business School, says, "The most empowering condition of all is when the entire organization is aligned with its mission, and people's passions and purpose are in sync with each other."[15]

Marilyn Carlson Nelson, former CEO and chairman of Carlson Companies, often speaks of the power and importance of her company's credo (mission). After planes crashed into the World Trade Center on September 11, 2001, Carlson Nelson set up an urgent conference call with employees in more than 150 countries. Her employees managed Radisson Hotels and Resorts around the world and serviced thousands of travelers through Carlson Wagonlit Travel. Planes were grounded, travelers displaced and afraid, and nothing was "business as usual."

On that day of uncertainty and fear, and with the potential of being disconnected from team members at any minute, not knowing for how long, Carlson Nelson shared the following:

"Our instructions are simple: take care of each other. Take care of our customers. Take care of our competitors' customers. Take care of your communities. Finally, if we lose communication, we authorize each of you to act according to the company credo. If you make decisions based on the credo, you won't be criticized for the results of your decisions."

The result of gathering everyone around the credo was alignment. People became creative, imaginative, and empowered by that simple instruction. It would have been an impossible task for Carlson Nelson to come up with solutions for organizing all her employees on 9/11. But they didn't need to be organized. They were aligned to a shared purpose and carried it out in the days after the catastrophe in ways that exceeded expectations of customers and made her proud.

What do you think would happen in your organization if there was a critical incident that caused a loss of direct contact with your various departments or divisions? Would everyone continue to operate according to the mission and vision? Or would there be an immediate decline in productivity and results due to a lack of alignment?

According to an article from Human Resource Development Quarterly, "Organizational alignment is the degree to which an organization's design, strategy and culture are cooperating to achieve the same goals. It is a measurement of the relative distance between several elements of organizational life. The strongest possible alignment will indicate the greatest probability of attaining the organization's strategic goals."[16] Organizational alignment is a key source of competitive advantage. But first, its elements must be measured.

Achieving a level of alignment that makes a positive impact on performance requires the determination of a starting point. That starting point involves measuring alignment across the nine pillars. Each of the pillars, as we've noted previously, are independent, yet they impact each other. As an example, with an increase in development, there's an increased probability of enhanced creativity among individuals. Increases in those two will impact accountability.

The process of measuring the pillars is simple and requires little time. Once the measurements are analyzed, it can become obvious what actions are required to create an increase in the selected metrics. These results are predicated on implementing strategies that get everyone focused on the mission and vision, increasing leadership capacity to lead in an aligned manner, as well as committing to an increase in accountability, empowerment, and teamwork.

Achieving a level of alignment that makes a positive impact on performance requires the determination of a starting point. That starting point involves the measurement of the nine pillars of alignment shown in the left column of the chart.

The process of measuring the pillars is simple and requires little time. Once the measurements are analyzed, it can become obvious what actions are required to create an increase in the selected performance metrics. These results are predicated on implementing strategies that get everyone focused on the mission and vision, as well as committing to an increase in accountability, empowerment, and teamwork.

PILLARS	BENEFITS DERIVED FROM ALIGNMENT
Mission and Vision	• Greater connection to purpose • Lower turnover • Greater communication and creativity
Leadership	• More effective execution of strategic plan • Better cross-team performance • Greater clarity and accountability
Communication	• Stronger ties to mission and vision • Empowerment levels increase • Creativity and best practices fostered
Accountability	• Engagement increases • Hopefulness increases • Chronic absenteeism declines
Empowerment	• Greater accountability to do best work • Less need for useless bureaucracy • Greater efficiencies for org and customers
Teamwork	• Siloes are eliminated • Efficiency increases • Best practices are continually upgraded
Creativity	• Innovation increases • Buy-in to new plans is enhanced • Fear of rejection of ideas decreases
Best Practices	• Greater creativity across organization • Growth mindset enhanced • Communication to generate ideas increased
Development	• Employees become more capable • Loyalty to company increases • A growth culture permeates

Remember the example of sailing from Hawaii to Los Angeles? With a 10-foot change in course every 100 feet, you could end up 250 miles from your destination. It's possible that your organization is only a few degrees out of alignment and that minor changes are all that's required to create an increase in your performance metrics.

- What if a one-point improvement in accountability could reduce absenteeism in schools by 28 percent, thus increasing graduation rates?
- What would happen if a simple change in communication could reduce readmission rates in hospitals by as much as seven percent?
- How might a five percent increase in creativity impact the next-level innovations your company is striving for in order to remain competitive in your marketplace?

By asking the right questions around the topic of alignment, organizations can, in essence, create something akin to the Staples Easy Button® when it comes to developing and implementing highly effective strategic plans. To over-simplify the process, here's the thinking, "We want this as our end result. Where are we starting from? And what's the roadmap we need to follow to get there?" At Medtronic, this process took the aggregate initial alignment score from the mid-50s to the mid-80s. Once the team was better aligned, it was able to accomplish that 13% year-over-year growth in a flat market.

Your initial path to higher performance could be as simple as presenting and discussing the mission and vision of your organization in every meeting. Or, it could be something else just as simple. You won't know until you assess the key elements of alignment.

When leaders are open to and in agreement with evaluating the level of alignment within their organizations through the strength of the defined constructs, room is made for improvement. New thinking occurs. Different ways of communicating are explored. Creativity is enhanced, and innovation abounds. There's a new level of excitement as leaders and individuals all work toward constant improvement in processes, keeping the end result of benefiting all stakeholders in mind. It's a beautiful thing. All oars are in the water, and everyone is pulling toward the same goal.

Self-Assessment

Now, it is time to reflect on your own organization. As you think through the strategic priorities this year, what are your top three priorities?

1. _____
2. _____
3. _____

Next, look back at the nine pillars of alignment and evaluate where your attention as a leader needs to be focused next quarter. As you get to work on one or more of these pillars, you will see that many of the issues you face are impacted for the better. The Nine Pillars of Alignment chart above outlines three common impacts from improvement in each of the nine pillars.

By clearly identifying the problems in your organization, the solutions become abundantly clear using a research-based approach to guide your leadership priorities.

The health of an organization is expressed in its strength of harmony between strategy, structure, and culture. These components come together in an organizational concept defined as alignment. Alignment is measured by the nine Pillars, providing leading indicators of key performance objectives. An assessment of alignment to these pillars gives any leader a non-judgmental baseline read on where the areas of occlusion exist, as well as the underlying circumstances.

A playbook of activities to remedy misalignment can range from the establishment of affinity groups to a forensic deep dive on diversity, equity, and inclusion and everything in between. We've discussed many ways you can lead in a more aligned manner within these pages. Best practices can be gleaned internally from effective feedback loops or external benchmarking. This playbook represents the action items pre-scribed to move the organization from misalignment to a more aligned state.

Every organization is different, with different capabilities and challenges. The work of getting a baseline read and putting a plan in place is elementary. Execution of the plan requires real, consistent, and intentional leadership. Correlating action to outcome is the special sauce that moves organizations into the space of the art of alignment. Take the time to understand where your organization is today, build your own leadership capabilities as well as those around you, and watch how per-formance improves as alignment increases.

I'm confident that this information can be used to make you a better leader and have a dramatically higher impact within your organization. Within all of us, there is an inherent untapped capability to create greater alignment with the mission. By creating greater alignment, you will release better products/services more quickly, out-perform your team scores, and, ultimately, fulfill the vision of your organization. Now it's time for you to put this information to good use and get aligned!

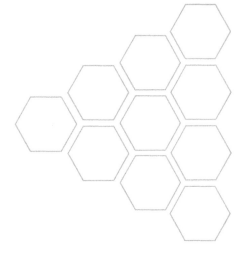

EPILOGUE

Throughout this book, I've described how establishing a baseline read of organizational alignment and building core fundamental leadership practices in the Nine Pillars of Alignment can not only improve performance, but do it in such a way that ties to metrics that matter to you.

Our work has unearthed a trove of data that helps organizations better understand what drives misalignment. Individuals who feel disenfranchised find it difficult to coalesce around the mission and vision of their employers. We hear statements from the disenfranchised such as "That is *their* vision" or "Our common values don't apply to me." I've seen first-hand, in my own experience, as well as with our clients, how underrepresented groups (e.g., people of color, LBGTQ, gender non-male, etc.) are much more likely to be significantly misaligned. Being part of an underrepresented group has given me the understanding of how organizations, and society in general, have treated us—causing us to become much more disconnected from our purpose at work and in our lives.

Diversity, equity, and inclusion (DE&I) is a critical component of becoming an aligned organization. Besides simply being the right thing to do, bringing forth more cultural competency through DE&I efforts improves every single one of our alignment pillars. The different experiences and insights brought from diversity improve communication and creativity. Best practices are enhanced. Leadership is trusted more because they are making the commitment to *all* employees. Leadership development naturally occurs because the organization works diligently to practice proper techniques across the organization. Accountability and empowerment are raised because of the energy that is created from these underrepresented groups. It also builds connection to your mission and vision because those who stay are committed to the positive energy in the environment; those who don't want to be part of the diversity will be low performers.

To address the need to assess how organizations are committed to DE&I, we decided to build an instrument that could obtain unbiased, normative data so organizations can improve their overall performance. Just like with our Orgametrics® score with alignment, a higher Equimetrics® score denotes greater cultural competency around DE&I.

Given the appetite to level the playing field for everyone, organizations are quickly seeing the value of the return on their cultural competency investment. They are seeing how greater DE&I directly translates to greater alignment with the mission and vision, hence greater levels of performance.

The global events of 2020 have put into stark relief the inequities in organizations, and society in general, that need to be addressed and rectified in order to move forward in productive ways. Greater DE&I raises the tide and all boats. Those organizations that commit to doing it well, and in a data-driven manner, will propel themselves into exponential levels of performance.

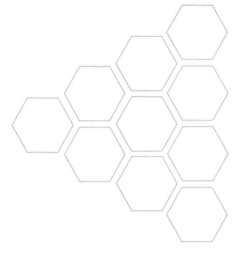

ENDNOTES

1. *Systematic Agreement: A Theory of Organizational Alignment* published in *Human Resource Development Quarterly, Human Resource Development Quarterly*, v8 n1 p23-40 Spr 1997

2. The One Minute Manager, Ken Blanchard and Spencer Johnson, William Morrow 2003

3. https://blog.clearcompany.com/why-aligning-corporate-goals -takes-more-than-just-software

4. Towers Watson. (2010). *Capitalizing on Effective Communication: Communication ROI Study Report.* Towers Watson

5. Yazdani, B. O., Yaghoubi, N. M., &Giri, E. S., (2011). Factors affecting the Empowerment of Employees. European Journal of Social Sciences, 20 (2), 267-274

6. IOSR Journal of Business and Management (IOSR-JBM) e-ISSN: 2278-487X, p-ISSN: 2319-7668. Volume 21, Issue 10. Series. V (October. 2019), PP 09-13. http://www .iosrjournals.org/iosr-jbm/papers/Vol21-issue10/Series-5 /B2110050913.pdf

7. https://www.nobelprize.org/womenwhochangedscience/stories/frances-arnold

8. https://www.aboutamazon.com/working-at-amazon/career-choice

9. Dr. Laurence J Peter and Raymond Hull, *The Peter Principle: Why Things Always Go Wrong*. Harvard Business, Revised Edition, 2011

10. *Ibid.*

11. Gino Wickman, *Traction*, BenBella Books, Inc. 2012

12. *Ibid.*

13. *JAMA Network Open.* 2019;2(5):e194270. doi:10.1001/jamanetworkopen.2019.4270 https://www.newsweek.com/people-sense-purpose-live-longer-study-suggests-1433771#:~:text=People%20With%20a%20Sense%20of%20Purpose%20Live%20Longer%2C%20Study%20Suggests,-By%20Kashmira%20Gander&text=People%20who%20have%20a%20sense,better%20physical%20and%20mental%20health.

14. 2018 workforce report, https://hr.az.gov/sites/default/files/2018%20Advisory%20Rec.pdf

15. "True North" by Bill George and Peter Sims pub Jossey-Bass 2007

16. Steven Semler above. *Human Resource Development Quarterly,* v8 n1 p23-40 Spr 1997

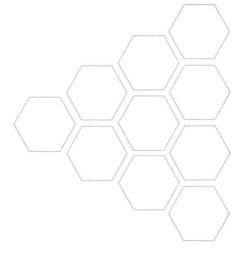

ABOUT THE AUTHOR

Art Johnson, CEO and founder of Infinity Systems, spent 25 years as a leader in the corporate world before launching his business. He led successful teams as an executive in Fortune 500 companies including IBM, USWest Communications and Medtronic.

Art was responsible for executing a strategic plan and had HR tools that measured engagement. Even with these robust tools, they were not able to measure how any of the data was impacting business performance. These tools were costly and time-consuming. Motivated to lead more effectively, Art developed the approach in this book to employee alignment.

Art holds a Bachelor's from Drake University, an MBA from the University of St. Thomas and he participated in the Executive Development Program at The Wharton School of Business.